THE MIND:

The Playground of the Devil

by

Pastor David L. Love

authorHOUSE™

1663 LIBERTY DRIVE, SUITE 200
BLOOMINGTON, INDIANA 47403
(800) 839-8640
WWW.AUTHORHOUSE.COM

© 2005 Pastor David L. Love. All Rights Reserved.
No part of this book may be reproduced, stored in a retrieval system, or transmitted by any means without the written permission of the author.

First published by AuthorHouse 02/03/05

ISBN: 1-4208-2906-8 (sc)

Printed in the United States of America
Bloomington, Indiana

This book is printed on acid-free paper.

Dedication:

    This book is dedicated to those people of God that would like to know how to resist the devil out of their minds and be set free of the devil and his mind games. We will take a step by step journey through the Bible and see how you can fight and win this battle of the mind. And it is dedicated to Jesus the One who has led me through this book. And my dear and devoted wife, Renee, who has stood by my side through two books, "Be a God Pleaser" and then this one, "The Mind: The Playground Of The Devil". May God bless all who read these books.

Contents

Introduction:

The great need for the Christian men and women of today is to know how that they can fight the battle of the mind and win through our Lord and Savior Jesus Christ and take back what the devil has stolen. We can take back our health, take back our marriage, take back our finances, take back our children, and don't allow the devil to use your mind as a playground, take back what is yours' in Jesus name. If you resist the devil he will flee from you. Come and learn how to be set free from the devil's tools he uses against you.

Chapter One:
The Battle Of The Mind
2 Cor. 10:3-5

We as Christians and well as the ungodly live in a world that has just gone wild. And I through the Spirit of God wa nt to tell you exactly where the problem is. The problem today is in the thought life of the people of this generation.

In Genesis 6 verse 5, we read, And God saw that the wickedness of man was great in the earth, and that every imagination of the thoughts of his heart was only evil continually . God sees all of the wickedness that is among us today, it cannot be concealed from him now or ever, and if it is not repented of, it will be revealed by Him shortly.

What was it that God took notice of? God observed all the streams of sin that flowed in men's lives, and breadth and depth of those streams. God saw that the wickedness of man was great in the earth. God observed the fountain of sin that was in men's hearts. Anyone could see that the wickedness of man was great, for it was declared as the sin of Sodom, but our Lord's eye went further. God saw that every imagination of the thoughts of his heart was only evil continually. It was a sad sight, very offensive to the Lord's holy eyes.

This indeed was the bitter root, the corrupt spring, lust conceived in them…. James 1:15 and Matt 15:19…. Their principles were corrupt and their habits and dispositions evil. And the thoughts of their heart were even so. Thoughts are sometimes taken for settled judgment or opinion, and these were as bribes, misleading, these were always vain or vile, weaving the spiders web or hatching the cockatrice's egg.

They did evil deliberately and designedly, contriving how to do mischief. It was bad indeed, for it was only evil, continually evil, every

1

imagination was so. There was no good to be found among them, not at no time, and the stream of sin was at full force and strong and constant, and God saw it. Ps.14:1-3.

This is an area in our Christian walk that we need God to take total control of. And we see that God destroyed an entire world because the imagination of their heart and of their thoughts was only evil continually.

Children of God, most or all of our battles as Christians are either won or lost in the mind. And what you think is vital to your success as a Christian man and woman. The book of Proverbs 23:7 says, As he thought in his heart, so is he. It's our thoughts that influences our attitudes, and our attitudes affects our actions and, yes, our actions become habits and habits become lifestyle. This is why the devil wants control of our minds. For he knows that if he can use your mind as a playground he can defeat us and bring us into bondage.

You have heard the saying you give the devil an inch and he will take a mile… well, that's true, don't give him even that inch, resist the devil and he will flee from you.

Child of God, have you ever had any of these thoughts? "I can't live the Christian life. I can't live in victory. The people in the church just don't love me. I don't feel like I am saved therefore I must not be saved. I can't overcome my bad habits." And the list goes on and on.

It seems every time someone in certain families go to the doctor, there is always someone in the family that thinks the worst. Did you know there are some people in the church that live their lives in defeat because this is the way they think.

Let me point out some things from this passage of scripture. The work of the ministry is warfare, not after the flesh, for it is spiritual warfare, with real spiritual enemies and for spiritual purposes. And though ministers and Christians live in the body, and in common affairs of life act as other men, but in the spiritual work and warfare we must not go by the acts of the flesh, nor should we design to please the flesh, nor entertain the fleshly mind thoughts. For this must be crucified with all of its affections and lust, it must be mortified and kept under submission to the Holy Spirit.

Saints of God ,oppositions are made against the gospel by the powers of sin and Satan in the hearts of men. Lusts, prejudices, ignorance, are Satan's strong- holds in the souls of some, vain imaginations, carnal reasoning, and high thoughts, or proud conceits, in others, exalt themselves against the knowledge of God, that is, by these ways the devil endeavors to keep men and women from the faith and obedience to the gospel, and secures his possession of the hearts of men and women, as his own house or property.

But we must observe the conquest which the word of God gains. Those strong-holds are pulled down by the gospel of God accompanying it as the principal efficient cause. Though we walk in the flesh we do not war after the flesh, this warfare is spiritual. You and I are given weapons in which to fight this war. We have weapons that are not carnal, they are not physical. We have weapons that are mighty, they are very powerful and our weapons are useful, they serve a mighty purpose.

Paul was telling us that this war was fought in the mind, in verse five. With this in mind, let me show you from the bible how to win the battle of the mind and gain control of your thoughts. Let me show you from the bible what kind of mind a person must have to win the battle of the mind.

You and I must have a saved mind (2Cor.4:3-4). Our mind, before salvation, was darkened and desensitized or beyond feeling because of our sinful nature. And you and I should not allow the devil to try and use our mind and try to desensitized us and start using our mind as his playground. Because if the devil can't get you one way, he will try and get to you through your mind and we must not allow it.

The god of this world will try and blind your mind, he will try to put you under his influence and power, but the word of God tells me... greater is he that lives within me than he that is in the world, my God is greater.

Before our salvation, our mind was darkened, beyond feeling because of our sinful nature, Ephesians.4:17-19... "This I say therefore, and testify in the Lord, that ye henceforth walk not as others Gentiles walk, in the vanity of their mind, Having the understanding darkened, being alienated from the life of God through the ignorance that is in them, because of the blindness of their heart: Who being past feeling have given themselves over unto lasciviousness, to work all uncleanness with greediness."

As Christians we must not live and behave as ignorant and unconverted heathens do, who are guided by an understanding employed about vain things, things which are no way profitable to our souls and which will deceive our expectations. We as converted Gentiles must not live as unconverted Gentiles do. Though we live among them we must not live like them.

Then in 2 Cor.4:3-4... "if our gospel be hid, it is hid to them that are lost: In whom the god of this world hath blinded the minds of them which believe not, lest the light of the glorious gospel of Christ who is the image of God, should shine unto them."You and I have a new mind set free through Jesus Christ, the devil, at one time, had us blinded to the gospel of the Lord.

One day the Lord reached down and removed the blinders from our eyes, allowed us to see the light of the gospel of God's saving grace. By the grace of our Lord and Savior we were saved and given a new mind. However, our mind has to be developed through prayer, bible study and regular church attendance.

This is why so many Christians today are being attack through the mind, because they do not have a daily diet of the word, prayer, and when the church doors are open they are not there. And thus the devil has a lead way directly into the mind of those people, we must apply these daily to our lives in order to overcome the enemy.

1 Pet.2:9 says…."you are a chosen generation, a royal priesthood, an holy nation, a peculiar people; that ye should show forth the praises of him who hath called you out of darkness into his marvelous light." When our Lord Jesus saved us we were called out of the darkness of sin that the devil had us in, into the glorious light of the Lord Jesus Christ. We no longer live in darkness for we are now the children of The Light.

When we have a saved mind, it is a mind that has been transformed and renewed by the power of the Holy Ghost. Let's look at a few passages of scriptures that reveal this truth to us. Rom.12:1-2… "I beseech you therefore, brethren, by the mercies of God, that ye present your bodies a living sacrifice, holy, acceptable unto God, which is your reasonable service. And be not conformed to this world: but be ye transformed by the renewing of your mind, that ye may prove what is that good, and acceptable, and perfect, will of God."

Eph.4:22…"That ye put off concerning the former conversation the old man which is corrupt according to the deceitful lusts;" verse 23 … "And be renewed in the spirit of your mind;" v.24… "And that ye put on the new man, which after God is created in righteousness and true holiness." v.25… "Wherefore putting away lying, speak every man with his neighbor: for we are members one of another."V.26… "Be ye angry, and sin not: let not the sun go down upon your wrath:" v.27… "Neither give place to the devil."

We as Christians must not give into the devils games,because he will use your mind if you allow him to as a playground to destory you and your walk with Jesus. For we are a new person in Jesus Christ, we are a new man/woman, and we must not allow the devil to tell us anything different. For we have royal blood flowing through our bodies, a King's blood, King Jesus, for we are King's kids.

Did you know when you got saved God gave us the mind of Christ? He did! Therefore we now possess the mind of Christ. 1 Cor.2:16 tells me… "For who hath known the mind of the Lord, that he may instruct him? But we have the mind of Christ." We are to be controlled by the mind and thoughts of the Lord Jesus Christ. But it is up to us to allow the mind of Christ to control us, its our choice… the ball is in our court, for in Phil.2:5 says… "Let this mind be in you, which was also in Christ."

You can overcome what the devil is trying to do to your mind, just think upon the things of God. Phil.4:8 says…"whatsoever things are true, whatsoever things honest, whatsoever things are just, whatsoever things are pure, whatsoever things are lovely, whatsoever things are of good report; if there be any virtue, and if there be any praise, think on these things."

And as Christians we must be single minded. For it says in 2Cor.11:13… "But I fear, lest by any means, as the serpent beguiled Eve through his subtlety, so your minds should be corrupted from the simplicity that is in Christ."

The word "simplicity" means… single-minded devotion or to be sincere. There are many that call themselves Christians who are not single- minded or sincere in their relationship with God. We have been corrupted from a single-minded devotion to Christ and are no longer sincere to Him.

Acts.5:3 Peter said… "Ananias, why hath Satan filled thine heart (mind) to lie to the Holy Ghost, and to keep back part of the price of the land?"

It really amazes me just how many Christians today allow Satan to rule their thought life with negative and destructive thoughts. It's amazing how many Christians think the worst about someone or something without knowing the facts or the truth.

Jesus said… "they draw nigh unto me with their lips but their hearts, (minds) are far from me." Today in our society there are so many people using lip service, saying I am a child of God, but in their hearts and mind they are not what they claim to be. If we confess with our lips that we are a Christian, our hearts and our mind will show it and line up with the word of God. People talk the talk but a lot fail to walk the walk.

In the book of Matthew.15:8 it says…. "This people draweth nigh unto me with their mouth, and honoureth me with their lips; but there heart is far from me."

In the book of Matthew.6:24 it says…. "No man can serve two masters: for either he will hate the one, and love the other, or else he will hold to the one, and despise the other. Ye cannot serve God and mammon {world}."

The choice is up to us to whom we will serve, but you cannot serve the Lord and the devil at the same time, it does not work that way. We must choose this day in whom we will serve. The Almighty God does not force himself on us. He loves us and wants us to serve Him. But God never forces himself upon no one, its our choice! Don't allow the devil to deceive you into believing a lie.

Paul was a single-minded man devoted to the Lord Jesus Christ. Philippians.3:13…. "Brethren, I count not myself to have apprehended: but this one thing I do, forgetting those things which are behind, and reaching forth unto those things which are before." V.14… "I press toward the mark for the prize of the high calling of God in Christ Jesus."

As Christians we need to follow Paul's example and be a single-minded man/woman, devoted to the King of Kings and Lord of Lords, and press on toward that mark for the prize of the high calling of God in Christ Jesus. To do our very best for Him, because He did His very best for us, on the cross that we could be saved and delivered from the strong holds of the enemy.

We also must have a mind that is sanctified, 2 Cor.10:4-5…. "For the weapons of our warfare are not carnal, but mighty through God to the pulling down of strong holds. Casting down imaginations, and every high thing that exalteth itself against the knowledge of God, and bringing into captivity every thought to the obedience of Christ."

We must use the weapons that our Lord and God has given unto us to pull down the strongholds that are in our minds. You may be asking, what is a stronghold? A stronghold is a thought or pattern of thoughts that keeps us from being everything the Lord God wants us to be or hinders the work that God has called us into for our life.

A stronghold is a fortified dwelling place. A stronghold can also be a source of protection for us as Christians from the devil. Psalm 18:2 states…. "The Lord is my rock, and my fortress, and my deliverer; my God, my strength, in whom I will trust; my buckler, and the horn of my salvation, and my high tower."

On the other hand, the stronghold can be a safe dwelling place for the devil to operate from. When Paul was speaking of pulling down strongholds, he is telling us to use the weapons that our Lord God has given us to destroy Satan's dwelling place in our minds that allows him to safely operate in our lives. If we pull down these strongholds Satan has no place from which he can operate.

We can have negative thoughts, sinful thoughts, greedy thoughts, lustful thoughts. Some may object by saying... I can't stop those negative and destructive thoughts from entering my mind. No, you can't. You can't stop a eagle from flying over your head either but you don't have to let that eagle build a nest in your hair. We are to take every thought captive and bring it into active obedience and submission unto the Lord Jesus Christ before it finds a resting place in our minds.

We MUST destroy these strongholds in our minds. As Christians we are to have the mind of Christ. We are to think God's thoughts or godly thoughts. Our weapons are: God's word, the Word of our testimony, prayer, the blood of Jesus... just to name a few.

As Christians we MUST have a surrendered mind unto Christ! 2 Cor.10:5... "Casting down imaginations, and every high thing that exalteth itself against the knowledge of God, and bringing into captivity every thought to the obedience of Christ."

We know that Ananias surrendered his mind to Satan and look at what it got him.... it got him dead, along with his wife.

We MUST surrender our minds to the Lord Jesus Christ and ALLOW Him to control what goes on in our minds.

There is steps to winning the battle of the mind. As Christians we need to admit our dependency upon God. James 4:10- KJV... "Humble yourselves in the sight of the Lord, and he shall lift you up." And the New Living Translation says... "When you bow down before the Lord and admit your dependence on him, he will lift you up and give you honor."

And we must, as children of God, submit to the authority and the will of our Lord and Savior Jesus Christ. James 4:7.... "Submit yourselves therefore to God, resist the devil, and he will flee from you."

We must commit our works unto God. Proverbs 16:3... "Commit thy works unto the Lord, and thy thoughts shall be established."

If we are going to win the battle of the mind then we must have a converted {saved} mind. We must also realize that a converted mind can be corrupted from it's single- minded devotion to the Lord Jesus Christ. A corrupted mind can be conquered and controlled, if we will use our God given weapons, to destroy the thought patterns that are contrary to the word of God and His will for our lives. And then surrender the control of our minds to God in total obedience.

Chapter Two:
How You Can Make Up Your Mind
James. 1:5-11

I want you to look at what James has to say about how you can make up your mind. Life, it is so full of decisions. Life is basically a series of choices we make every day. We have to decide, draw conclusions, and evaluate things. Did you know that your life is a result of the decisions you make? YES! The quality of our lives will be determined by the kind of decisions we make in life. Some of them we regret and some of them we feel good about.

Because we are human we all have a very great possibility for error. A lot of times we wait too long, we pay too much, we even say the wrong thing. You could be making a difficult decisions this very day. And some don't even know it yet but you could have a major decision tomorrow. Life is full of choices.

James tells us about how to make decisions. How do we make up our mind? James gives us the problem and then he gives us the prescription. Then he also gives us the promise from the Lord and then the position in which we are to place ourselves in.

The Problem? Indecision... V. 8 says.... "a double- minded man is unstable in all his ways." In the Greek, double- minded literally means two souls pulled apart in different directions, divided priorities. James speaks the word but we have felt that way once or twice in our life- when we are trying to do two things at one time. We really are not sure of what we want.

We have to make a decision. When you are double-minded it can be devastating, because it makes you very unstable. The word is translated "confused" in many parts of the Bible. It's used to describe a drunk who's staggering, reeling, unstable in all his ways. He's saying, If you can't make up your mind it produces an unstable lifestyle. All your ways will be unstable. Constant turmoil.

There are at least three ways indecision can make you unstable. One is unstable emotions.

It's a strain when you can't decide. You worry and are strained, you are confused. You can't eat or sleep. Then you began to wonder, did I do the right thing? It will create emotional instability in your life when you can't make up your mind, and that is just what the enemy wants to do to your mind, but you don't have to allow it, not one little bit.

Two is unstable relationships. Lack of commitment destroys marriages when we can't decide. Do I want in or do I want out? What must I do here? It's instability in relationships. Are you unstable on the job and switching back and forth between careers? Are you a parent who says one thing, then you change your mind and say another thing? We often give double messages to our children and it causes instability in their lives as well. Some can't decide in a relationship. Am I going to get out of this relationship or am I going to get on with it. I have discovered many times it takes more of our energy deciding than it does to just do it. But the once you do it, it's a snap, but the key is deciding.

The devil will try and mess us up in all our decisions if we allow him to. See the mind is where the devil loves to play. He will use our mind as his playground and mess with our decision making and we will become unstable in all our ways. Don't allow the devil to interfere with your relationships, lack of commitment, your career, your family, or your Christian walk with the Lord. Tell the devil to take a hike! That you are a King's kid and that you have the royal blood, Christ's blood flowing through your body, and you have the mind of Christ. Then you will get the devil on the run. Praise God!

We can also have an unstable spiritual life. James1:7......"For let not that man think that he shall receive anything of the Lord." An unstable spiritual life can block your prayer life and your prayers. Indecision keep God from giving you the desires of your heart and it will keep you from receiving what the Lord has to offer you in all areas of your Christian walk with Him. And this is just what the devil wants to do to you. The devil don't care how much you read the word of God or how much you go to church, as long as he can hold you back from receiving the spiritual things that God wants to give you. God can't give you those things you need and desire because the devil has made you unstable and he is working on your mind with indecision, and therefore you have a unstable spiritual life. Do not allow this to take place friend.

You may be saying at this point why doesn't God answer my prayers? Could it be that you are not specific enough. Or maybe you have never really decided what it is you really want God to do and you really don't have a clear cut goal about it. Don't allow the devil to keep you from receiving what God wants to give you. For the word of God says you have not because you ask not. We I have to be specific on what we ask God for. And the devil will try and get you to the point where you are not specific enough and that you do not have a clear cut goal for what you are about to ask God for. The devil will play with your mind. He will try and use your mind as his playground if you allow him to. Double- mindedness can lead to a double life like a Dr. Jekyll & Mr. Hyde or Mr. Facing-Both-Ways. That is when you want to do your will and God's will at the same time. The bible says you can not serve two masters.

When we know what's right but we do wrong any way, it's a sin and the devil loves it. Don't allow the enemy to deceive you in to believing a lie. When you are trying to live two ways it just doesn't work out…. period! On Sunday you sing "When the Roll Is Called Up Yonder I'll Be There" and on Monday you are "AWOL" from walking with God. Double-mindedness will produce a double- life. It will cause instability in all of your ways. It produces an unstable life style. Don't allow the enemy to use your mind as his playground to tell you "it's ok to live this way", because it is a lie from the devil. The devil knows if he can't get you in one way, he will play with your mind and try to get you in another way.

But there is a prescription you have that you can use. Ask God for help. The problem could very well be indecision. You may say what's the solution? James makes it clear, get wisdom. "If any of you lacks wisdom you should ask God who gives generously to all without finding fault and it will be given to him." We as Christians should not be afraid to ask our Lord for help in any area of our lives, and if we need more wisdom, ask God who gives wisdom to those of us that will only ask. And don't allow the devil to keep us back from asking our heavenly Father. For we can call upon our daddy, Abba Father, for we are His children.

James gives us three practical steps that we can follow. One… we should admit our need. V. 5… "if any of you lack wisdom"….if any of us don't have it all together. The book of James is the book of wisdom in the New Testament. Just like Proverbs is the book of wisdom in the

Old Testament. If you will be true to yourself, you know that you may be lacking wisdom. It is universal. We all lack wisdom. Wisdom is very different from knowledge. Wisdom is knowledge put into practice. Wisdom is truly seeing life from God's point of view. Wisdom is making decisions the way (and only this way) God would make decisions. The Bible speaks a lot about wisdom. But most people all they are interested in is the head knowledge. This world is impressed with head knowledge. But God is impressed with us using spiritual wisdom from Him. What is it that you do with your knowledge? Do you put it into practice and make use of it? Wisdom, my friend, is the ability to make decisions the way God would want use to make decisions…. His way. The devil is trying to play with our minds so that we will not ask God for wisdom. Don't allow it to happen.

Proverbs.11:2… "When pride cometh, then cometh shame (disgrace): but with the lowly wisdom." Pride blocks wisdom. We can't learn anything if we think we know it all! One of the main reasons why we never learn wisdom is we think that we have it all together and figured out. God's word is saying… admission of the lack of wisdom is the beginning of wisdom. I truly don't have it all together and I don't have all the answers. For some of you men it may be hard for you to say to your wife…. I was wrong. When was the last time you said… I was wrong? It shows how wise you really are when you admit you are wrong. There is no shame or degradation in admitting you are wrong. The admission of lack of wisdom is the beginning of wisdom. I know I don't have all the answers. I don't even know all the questions. But the key to wisdom is to start by saying… I really don't know God. What is it that you want me to do? Admit to God {and to others} that you don't have all the answers. And admit your need! Don't allow the devil to deceive your mind and use it as his playground.

The second one is to ask. Ask for wisdom. We need to pray to God about it… talk to Him. If any of you lack wisdom let him ask of God. How do you get wisdom? By listening to Dr. So & So ? By watching the TV? Taking smart pills? By reading magazines on "how- to"? The Bible says you get wisdom by asking God. That's where wisdom comes from….God. So we must talk with Him about it and ask for wisdom. Proverbs.2:6…. "For the Lord gives wisdom: out of his mouth comes knowledge and understanding." The way that we can receive wisdom is stop allowing the enemy in to play with our minds to the point that he has us on his merry-go-round and he is telling us a lie and keeping us back from asking God for spiritual wisdom in our lives.

Let me ask you… if our God was to come to you this day and say, "I'm going to give you one thing spiritual in your life. You can ask for anything in the whole world. You can have one thing." What would you ask for? There was one such man that got that chance in the Old Testament. God came to Solomon and said…"You're the king of Israel. I am going to grant you one thing. What do you want more than anything else in life?" Solomon thought it over and said, "I'm inadequate as a leader. I don't know what to do with these people. More than anything else I want wisdom. I want to be able to think the way you think to see things from your point of view, be able to make decisions the way you would make them. I don't want to make mistakes. Just give me wisdom." The Bible says God was pleased with that request. He granted it to him.

Just like God will always give wisdom to those that ask Him for it. He said Solomon, because you ask for wisdom, I'm going to give you other things to: wealth, fame, long life. Solomon not only became the wisest man, but he was the wealthiest man, a famous person, and he lived a long life. And is well-known throughout all the world.

God is trying to tell us that's how important wisdom is. Proverbs says…. if you don't get anything else… get wisdom. And the reason we don't have wisdom is we don't ask. James 4:2… "You have not because you ask not." This word in the Greek literally means: keep on asking, be persistent, be continual. And as a Pastor, I would not dare presume to lead the church without continually asking God for wisdom. I wouldn't presume to try to lead the church otherwise. It's not my church. It's God's anyway. The spiritual responsibility of the Shepherd is to discover what God wants to do in his body.

Thirdly, anticipate. Expect an answer in faith. We need to learn to anticipate an answer. When you pray, if any of you lack wisdom he should ask God who gives generously to all without finding fault and it will be given to him. But when we ask, we must believe and not doubt. If you want wisdom…first, you've got to ask the right person and that person is God. Then we have to ask the right way…in faith, believing, not doubting. The main key to wisdom is our prayer, and the condition is our faith. We can't allow the devil to keep our minds messed up to the point that we don't anticipate it, that we don't expect an answer in faith. Because the devil will play with your mind to the point that you don't believe, you just don't have the faith. Or you have the faith but the devil has brought forth doubt into your mind. Don't allow this to take place.

Let me ask you this…. have you ever prayed a prayer then later while talking to someone say, "But I knew I wouldn't get it." You have just set your self up for doubt, and you have allowed the enemy to steal your victory. God says… if you can't believe to get it, don't even waste the time praying for it. Because if you allow the devil to come into your mind while you are praying and bring doubt OR if you came to God with doubt already in your heart and mind you will not come forth in victory. But you must pray in faith, believing, thanking God in advance for the answer being given. Doubt is debilitating. It will hinder God from working in your life. So please don't allow the devil to use your mind as his tool and playground. Don't allow him to put doubt in, where Jesus has placed faith there. For we all, that are Christians, have a measure of faith that Christ has placed within us…. Rom.12:3.

This reminds me of Peter. Remember Peter was in the boat, Jesus comes walking on the water. Peter he jumps out and starts walking towards Jesus. (If you and I want to walk in real faith, we have to get out of the boat. We will have to take risks in life if we are going to live by faith. It doesn't require any faith to stay in the boat. We have to jump out of the boat and take that step of faith and then God will take care of us.) Peter starts walking across the water. He's got his eyes on the Lord. Then all of a sudden he looks down and thinks, "I'm not supposed to be able to do this." Instantly he starts to sink. The moment you get your eyes off of Jesus and lose faith in Him and look at the circumstance… you're dead-meat!

Some of you who are reading this book may have a major problem that you have to make a decision on, and the reason you don't have the answer to the decision you have to make is because you are looking at the problem and not the Lord. "This is a big problem. How will I ever solve it. I'm backed into a corner. It is impossible for me!" But let me say my God specializes in the impossible! Get your eyes off the problem, off the circumstances. And get your eyes on the Lord. For if you have your eyes on the problem you will sink! But you must believe and not doubt. He who doubts is like a wave of the sea, blown and tossed by the wind. A lot of Christians are like fishing bobbers in the ocean, blown around, back and forth. They become victims of their own circumstance. And some of you are blown away at this very moment because you haven't been asking the Lord for wisdom. And eventually you pray, as if prayer is the last resort. That ought to be the first option!

Hebews.11:6 says…. "But without faith it is impossible to please him: for he that cometh to God must believe that he is, and that he rewards them that diligently seek him." If you and I want to receive anything from God we have to believe in advance that we will get it. That's faith. Faith is thanking God in advance.

Wisdom is promised! God will give it! If any of you lack wisdom, let him ask of God, that will give to all men liberally, and upbraided not; and it shall be given. God wants to give you wisdom. He is eager to do so. Just like it pleased God when Solomon asked for wisdom, it pleases God when we come to Him and say, "I haven't a clue about what I am supposed to do" We just need to start asking God and kick the devil in the face, so all he can do is sputter! Stop allowing the devil to steal what God has for you. To those of us who believe, stop allowing the devil to use your mind as a playground. Put up a "NO TRESPASSING!" sign, and let the devil know you are the property of God and you have the mind of Christ. Ask God! It is God's nature to give. God is a giving God. Glory to God!

Proverbs 3:5-7 says…. "Trust in the Lord with all thy heart; and lean not unto thine own understanding. In all thy ways acknowledge him, and he shall direct thy paths. Be not wise in thine own eyes: fear the Lord and depart from evil."

Wisdom is applying the promise of God's word to your life and problems. Then allowing God to accomplish what he wants in your life through your trial. We need so very mush to tell the devil to take a hike! For we have the word of God! And all of God's promises are yes and Amen.

God says He'll give wisdom continually. We need to ask God who gives freely! In the Greek it is in the continuous tense. He keeps on giving. My God does not run out of energy. God never wears out. God gives generously His resources… they are unlimited. God has enough resources for everyone. He's a God of plenty. And all God is waiting on is you to release what's in your heart and mind, and that is faith to believe Him at His word. Then God will release what's in His hands unto you what's in his heart and mind for you at that appointed time. Don't allow the devil to make a playground of your mind so that you will not be able to receive what God has for you and your life.

God will also give unto you without insulting you. God gives to cheerfully. Have you ever received something from someone who you knew was giving it to you grudgingly and it took the joy out of it? They knew that they had to and there wasn't any joy in it. God does not give wisdom that way. God loves to give. It's in His nature to give. You and I need to never feel embarrassed. There should never be any hesitation. God does not resent your asking for wisdom. God is pleased when you come to him and ask Him for things that you need spiritually. Don't never allow the devil to put in your mind that you are not worthy to ask God for anything that you have need of, for God has made you worthy through his Son Jesus Christ. Resist the devil! Give him a big Holy Ghost punch and knock him out of your mind and then God will give you the desire of your heart.

We should be happy and pleased that it's God's nature to give to His children. Our God is our model for giving. And if we want to become more like God, we need to become giving people. For God wants us to give continually, generously, and cheerfully. That's what giving is all about. God says you give because I give.

Where do you need wisdom right now? What is the big decision that is facing you at this time in your life? Is it marriage? Is it a career decision? Church membership? Children? An investment? It's very interesting that James in chapter 1: 5-8 and 9-11, gives us a practical application of where we need wisdom. And of all the areas that James could have chosen to give as an example, he chose money. Why you might say? There are more people who make unwise decisions and foolish choices regarding their finances than almost anything in this world! There are so many people who are double-minded and unstable when it comes to money than any other area. I see so many Christians in financial bondage, because they are violating God's principles. We need to decide… have we made up our minds to love God and give in tithes and offerings and abide by God's principles and not our own? Don't allow the devil to cheat you out of the blessing of God and make a curse of things in your life by putting in your mind not to give to God and his work. Make the right decisions.

This is a fantastic promise here in the book of James chapter one, and all we have to do is claim it. There is a couple of things James is saying about decision making: God does not want to make the decisions for us that we should be able to make on our own. It does not say pray and God will make the decision for you. Otherwise, we would not mature in the Lord. God wants us to grow up. When God made man in Genesis chapter one, He made him in His image. Part of that image is free will. God gave us a lot of responsibility when He gave us the freedom to choose. God wants you and I to make the decisions, but based on His wisdom. He does not want to make them for us.

I have heard sincere Christians say, "I don't know what to do. So all I am going to do is leave it up to the Lord." That "sounds" spiritual. Sometimes that's exactly what you should do. Sometimes that's what God will tell you and I to do. But a lot of the times the phrase "I am going to leave it up to the Lord," is a cop-out. It's saying, I am scared to death. I am a poor decision maker. I really don't know which way to turn, therefore I am going to accept whatever happens and call it God's will. And the fact is, God's will is not always done. Everything that happens is not necessarily God's will for our lives. That is why we pray the Lords prayer, Thy will be done on earth as it is in Heaven. In Heaven, God's will is done perfectly. But it is not done perfectly here on earth. Because a lot of things are done that are not God's will because we make the wrong decision. We just let things go. And sometimes passivity is the exact opposite of what God wants us to do. God wants you and I to get on our knees and pray for wisdom until we KNOW the right thing to do. God wants us to make the decision. He will not make it for us. He wants us to grow up. Learn ourselves. Maturity in a Christian's life is making decisions the way Jesus would. And don't blame God for your indecisions.

God's wisdom is found in God's word. If we want wisdom we have to get into reading the word of God. We need to get on our knees, pray, and ask God to show us what to do. Give us wisdom Lord. Teach us principles that will apply in this situation. Then we need to read, study, memorize, and meditate on the word of God. God's wisdom is found in His Word. We need to be reading through the scriptures continuously. In Psalm.119:105 it says God's "word is a lamp unto our feet and a light unto our path." It shows us the way. Don't allow the devil to use your mind as his playground and tell you that you don't have to read or study God's word every day or pray every day. That is a lie that the devil is using on Christians today keeping them from the wisdom of Almighty God.

James is trying to tell us that we will live our life either by chance or choice. Either based on the circumstances where you're a victim of the circumstances and let everything bat you back and forth OR you will choose to make choices. For the quality of your life is determined by the choices you make and the wisdom that is behind those choices. James is saying when we do not trust in God it will produce a lifestyle of instability in our lives. The cause of all our frustrations in life is not our indecisions over our job, marriage, children or health… although those are important. But there is a deeper issue and that is our inability to trust God and to lay it all down at His feet and into His hands and ask for wisdom.

Where might you be double- minded? Where have you been wavering and trying to live two different ways, trying to live for the Lord on Sunday and then downplaying it during the week? This is what produces instability in our lives. And this is just how the enemy would want us to live and think. If he can make you believe a lie and put it in your mind and use it as a game against you he will, and then he will keep coming back to use your mind as his playground. So don't allow him to even start with your mind, because once it gets into your mind it will take residence up in your heart. Resist the devil and he will flee from you.

What is life's greatest decision? The greatest decision we could make in life is this: Who's going to be number one in our life? Are you going to be number one? Is your money number one? Is your family number one? Is your job number one? There is only one thing that will bring and produce stability in your life. And that is when God is number one in your life. No man can serve two masters. You will hate the one and love the other. The most important decision you could ever make would be to make Jesus Christ number one in your life. We need to say Lord you call the shots. You are the chairman of the board. And I will check in with you on a regular basis. You be my guide in this life. We need to give it ALL to the Lord Jesus Christ, and fight the devil that is trying to interfere with our minds in making us think that it is alright to put things before God. That's a lie from the devil! Don't allow it! Put Christ as the head, number one and all the rest shall be added unto you.

And in the close of this chapter, we must position our selves with humility (humble)…James 1: 9-10, 1 Peter.5:6, James.4:10, Rom.12:3. For in the book of 1 Peter.5:6 says: "Humble yourselves therefore under the mighty hand of God, that he may exalt you in due time." James.4:10 says: "Humble yourselves in the sight of the Lord, and He shall lift you up." Rom.12:3 says: "For I say, through the grace given unto me, to every man that is among you, not to think of himself more highly than he ought to think; but to think soberly, according as God hath dealt to every man the measure of faith." Dear reader and Christian friends we must not allow the devil to play with our minds, to the point that he is using our mind as his playground and keeping us back from humbling ourselves before the Lord God Almighty and keep us from asking our Father for wisdom in all areas of our lives.

Have the faith of God to believe, because without faith it is impossible to please God. Don't allow the devil to use your mind as his playground! Put a stop to it this day and take back what the devil has been stealing from you.

Chapter Three:
Hindrances To Thinking
God's Thoughts
1 Cor.2:9-16

So much of our lives are affected by the way we think? The true fact is, that everything that you and I are and everything that we do is driven by the way we think. If we want to change some behavior or action in our lives, just where do we begin? A change in behavior always begins with a great change in our mind, in the way that you and I think. It has been said that our attitude will determine our altitude. The key to victorious Christian living begins with learning how to take control of our thought life. How we think will determine how far we will go with God, how much we will grow spiritually, how much of His fullness we will experience, and how much of His life and peace we will enjoy.

Let's not allow the enemy to affect the way we think. Because the enemy will try and use our mind as his playground, and try to hinder us in thinking God's thoughts. Let's not allow this to happen in our mind. The Bible says to be carnally minded is death; but to be spiritually minded is life and peace. I don't think that you want to be carnally minded. I don't think you want the enemy to play with your mind to the point that you "lose out" spiritually. I do think that you want to be spiritually minded so that you can enjoy the spiritual life and the peace that Jesus gives us through thinking upon the things of God.

I want to share with you just a little on why we should develop the mind of Christ {which I will go into more detail in Chapter 15: Developing The Mind Of Christ}. There are several reasons why we as Christians should develop the mind of Christ. Most of our battles are won or lost in our mind. True life change MUST begin with a transformed mind. As a newborn Christian, we should possess the mind of Christ. We must CONSTANTLY choose between two opposing patterns of thought….. faith and reason. But this is a huge area where the enemy tries to come in through our minds and play games with it. Don't allow this to take place in your life.

Our thinking affects our perspective {our out look} on life, but by developing the mind of Christ we learn to view life and our circumstances from the Lord's perspective and not our own. Our thinking can affect our personality, because our thought patterns shape our personality. This is why, if you can begin to get the right perspective on life it won't be long until you will see your personality is transformed and you will become more like Jesus Christ in all areas of your life. Some of us really could use a personality transplant. You are what you think, as they say.

This is why the devil will come and try to use your mind as his playground because he does not want your mind transformed into the likeness of the Jesus Christ. Then he knows he'll lose the battle of the mind. Let's make the devil a loser, because that is just what he is… a Big loser. For we are the winners! We are in God's army and in Him there are no losses, it is all about victory in Jesus!!

Our thinking can also affect our priorities. We will give our mind to what ever is top priority in our lives. Our priorities are heavily influenced by the world around us. This is why we must check every thought with the bible and bring it into captivity and obedience to the Lord Jesus Christ. This is an area where the enemy likes to strike at in our minds… bringing every thought into captivity and obedience to the Lord. See the enemy knows how much that God respects obedience in all areas of our Christian lives and it comes right down even to our thought life. And this is where the enemy loves to strike at and play with us in. We must therefore fight back and resist the devil and he will flee from us. For we should truly want to be obedient in all areas of our Christian walk. And if we are obedient in our thought life we will be obedient in other areas of our life.

Our thinking can also affect our prayers. Much of our pray life is powerless, ineffective due to the fact that we are praying with the wrong motive or not praying according to God's will for our lives. We should be glad that God hasn't answered all of the selfish prayers that we have prayed. If we are going to be spiritually minded, which leads to life and peace, we will have to reject the thoughts of Satan and this old world and embrace the thoughts of God. God's thoughts are revealed in and through His word. God's word is His will for our lives. Don't allow the enemy to tell you not to pray, or to pray this way or that way. We must not submit to the thoughts that Satan try's to inject in our minds by playing mind games with us. Don't allow the enemy to use your mind as his playground and get you into believing a lie and keep you back from receiving a spiritual mind in Christ.

This is just what the devil wants for your life, that is, he does not want you to have the mind or thoughts of Christ. And if the devil can interject his thoughts into your mind to the point that he can make you stop praying like you should, stop reading the word like you should, or attending church like you should, then he knows just where to attack YOU… and that is through your thought life. Don't allow this to happen in your walk with the Lord. Rebuke the devil and resist him and he will have to flee from your mind, your thoughts and all areas of your spiritually life. Praise God!

If we as Christians are going to be victorious in our thought life, we must conquer the habit of wrong thinking. If you are a believer, if you have been born again, if you have been forgiven of your sins then you are a child of God and you possess the mind of Christ. He helps you to control the way you think. And if you are not a believer, and you are reading this book, if you haven't ask God into your life and to forgiven of your sins, you can do so today. And then you can possess the mind of Christ by believing in Him, and being born again. And today, you can begin to take control of your thoughts. So stop allowing the devil to put in your mind that you can't do this or that ,you tell him that you can because you are a child of God and you possess the mind of Christ. And then he can't tell you anything that will persuade you into believing anything different. For the way you live and the way you feel and your outlook on life will be transformed as your mind is transformed by the power and presence of a godly thought life… 1 Cor.2:16.

There are interferences to thinking godly thoughts. Why is it that so many Christians are unable to think right? Why do so many Christians have strongholds in their minds? Why are so many unable to control their thoughts? And what causes people in general, and specifically Christians, to think and be controlled by ungodly thoughts? What causes this disease of wrong thinking? What interferences keep so many of God's people from thinking godly and wholesome thoughts? I know two of the interferences that keep God's people from thinking godly and wholesome thoughts… external {outside} sources of interference and internal {inside} sources of interference.

External {outside} interferences to thinking godly and wholesome thoughts that I want us to identify and deal with are three external sources that interfere with our thinking and hinder us from thinking godly thoughts. Satan can interfere with you, he can interfere with your thinking and hinder you from thinking godly thoughts. 2 Cor.11:3… "But I fear, lest by any means, as the serpent beguiled Eve, through his subtlety, so your minds should be corrupted from the simplicity that is in Christ." Take a quick look at how Satan deceived Eve. And how Satan would love so very much as to do the same to you and I in using our minds as his playground. Satan introduced the thought to Eve that God is not the author of His word. Gen.3:1…"Yea, Hath God Said?" More in our terms…"Are you sure this is what God said?" This was questioning God's word.

The devil was saying to Eve, how do you know that you can trust the authorship and authenticity of God's word? And then the devil questioned the credibility of God. Gen.3:4…. "Ye shall not surely die". {God is lying to you. God said you would die but that's a lie; you will not die. How do you know you can trust God?} And then the devil questioned the character of God. Gen.3:5… "For God doth know that in the day ye eat thereof, then your eyes shall be opened, and ye shall be as gods, knowing good and evil". The devil was telling Eve, God is selfish and is keeping something from you to keep you from enjoying life. How do you know that you can trust God to give you what is best for your life?

The enemy will try his best to inject your mind with all kinds of thoughts that are not of God. And if you allow him, he will take your mind on a ride in his playground that will end up with you believing a lie that he has placed there. And the fact is that Satan and his demons CAN interfere with our thought life. Satan can definitely place thoughts in our mind. But it is up to us what we do with those thoughts. Do we entertain them? NO!! We resist them in the name of Jesus and put the devil on the run! There is no question that the enemy has access to your mind and he can plant his thoughts into your mind. { II Cor.4:4, Luke22:3, John13:27, II Cor.11:3, Luke 8:35, Acts 5:13} This is what we call Satan's deception. The great deception of Satan is when he can place his thoughts in your mind and leads you to believe they are YOUR thoughts.

See, if Satan can place a thought in your mind {and he can} it isn't much more of a trick for him to make you think it's your idea. For if you knew it was from Satan you would reject that thought, wouldn't you? But when he disguises his suggestions as your idea, you are more likely to accept it. That is his primary deception.

Satan CAN influence your mind and interfere with your capacity for thinking godly and wholesome thoughts. 1 Peter 5:8-9..." Be sober, be vigilant; because your adversary the devil, as a roaring lion, walketh about, seeking whom he may devour. Whom resist steadfast in the faith, knowing that the same afflictions are accomplished in your brethren that are in the world." And also Eph.4:27 says..." Neither give place to the devil"...in other words, do not give the devil a foothold to start with! See, the devil is seeking the minds of Christians and he is seeing if he can use your mind as his playground so that he my devour you and render you useless for the Lord. Don't give place to the devil my friend, resist him out of your thought life, don't let the enemy have a foothold on your mind.

The world also can interfere with our thinking and hinder us from thinking godly and wholesome thoughts. Rom. 12:2 says..." And be not conformed to this world: but be ye transformed by the renewing of your mind, that ye may prove what is that good, and acceptable, and perfect, will of God". The word "conformed" means "to press into a mold". The Apostle Paul is telling us... Don't be pressured into the mold of the world. Don't allow the world to influence the way you think. Don't let the world pressure you into thinking the way it thinks. The enemy would love nothing better than to use your mind as his playground, in trying to get you to conform to the way this world thinks and does things. But don't allow the enemy to press you into the mold of this world, and keep you back from thinking the thoughts of God. We must take charge of our own minds through the guidance of the Holy Spirit! For greater is He that is within us than he that is in the world! Praise God for the victory that we have in Jesus Christ and for the Holy Spirit that leads, guides, and directs our lives.

A great deal of our thought patterns, ideas, beliefs, values and attitudes are shaped by the world system and the culture that we live in. And there is a constant need for us to evaluate what is going on in our minds and thoughts, and weigh it against God's word. We are to use God's word to discern, whether this is from God or is this from the enemy and the world system in which I live in? All of us have been raised in this world filled with it's negative environment that is anti-Christ and godless. If you are about ready to make a decision in your life about a job, about children, about college, marriage, please base it upon God's Holy Word and not upon how you feel or think. Because a wrong decision is one that you could pay for the rest of your life! But a godly decision is ALWAYS the right decision. Don't allow the enemy to make the decisions for you by playing with your mind.

If you are a Christian, when you were born-again, God gave you a new nature and you became a new person. But no one has pressed the "clear button" in your brain. We still brought with us into this "new life" the Lord gave us.....all the habits and thought patterns that were developed and ingrained in our minds prior to our conversion. And we are still being bombarded with anti-Christ messages, philosophy, and values from the world in which we live, because ,while we are not of this world, we still live in the world. But praise God, we have the victory to overcome the things that the enemy is placing in our minds through our Lord Jesus Christ.

And we need to truly understand that everything we expose ourselves to will influence our minds and it will leave an impression there. The music we listen to. The people we fellowship with. The movies we watch. And the books we read. This is why we must be very careful in what we expose our minds to. As Christians we have to constantly filter out what we hear and what we see around us. How? Through the Holy Word of God, prayer, and by being very sensitive to the leadership of the Holy Spirit in our lives. Do not allow the enemy to attack your mind and to use it as his playground and to keep you back from receiving what the Holy Spirit of God is guiding you into.

And sometimes these thought patterns that develop from the influence of the godless environment around us can become strongholds. Strongholds defined: well -fortified place; fortress. An activity can quickly become a habit, and a habit can quickly become a stronghold. It's a process called "conditioning". The more we expose to the negative influences around us the more conditioned we become towards them. I have heard if you put a frog in hot water he will jump out. However, if you put him in a pan of cold water and turn on the fire he will stay in the water and be cooked to death.

Also our flesh can interfere with our thinking and hinder us from thinking godly and wholesome thoughts. Our flesh is that self-sufficient, self-centered part of us, which has been trained to live independently of God. When we became a Christian, we became a new creation, and the old man died, but the flesh remains a constant threat to our spiritual, mental, and emotional well-being. And this is why the bible wants us to be alert to our fleshly tendencies, and not to submit any longer to the impulses of the flesh. { John.8:15, Rom.8:1,4, Rom.8:12, 1 Cor.10:3.} Any time you have a desire to do anything independent of God, this is from our own flesh. Our flesh cries out for self-satisfaction. Our flesh seeks to act apart form God. And the enemy is good at placing things in our minds that our fleshly desires and are not godly desires and therefore we must resist the enemy and he will flee our minds.

We are told in the word of God that we are to no longer be controlled by our flesh, but by our spirit. Rom.8:9 says…" But ye are not in the flesh, but in the Spirit". As Christians we need to realize that greater is the Spirit of God that is with in us than the enemy that is in the world. We don't have to allow the enemy to control our thought life, because we have a greater power within us to fight the enemy and win. We are on the winning side! Praise God!

And then, child of God, there is internal {inside} interferences to thinking godly and wholesome thoughts. Let me just say that there are some mental conditions that we possess which interfere with our ability to think God's thoughts. I will list some of these harmful mental conditions which are spoken of in the word of God. One is a "darkened mind" that can interfere with thinking godly and wholesome thoughts. This describes the mental and spiritual condition of every unbeliever, of an unregenerate mind. And it describes someone who is spiritually dead, and unable to understand and grasp spiritual truth. {Eph.4:17-19}. And when a Christian is controlled by this mind set it's called in the word of God the "carnal mind". {Rom.8:6}. This describes a Christian that is being influenced by their fleshly nature. Thus they think and do those things that are influenced by the selfish desires of the old fleshly nature.

1 Peter.2:11…" Dearly beloved, I beseech you as strangers and pilgrims abstain from fleshly lust, which war against the soul." And this is why the world will not respond to the saving grace and message of the Lord Jesus Christ. The world lies in darkness….mental and spiritual darkness. They are controlled by the desires of the flesh. {2 Cor.4:4} The god of this age has blinded the minds of the unbelievers, so that they cannot see the light of the gospel of the glory of Christ, who is the image of God. This was our condition prior to our conversion to the Lord Jesus Christ. Eph.2:3… "Among whom also we all had our conversation in times past in the lust of our flesh, fulfilling the desires of the flesh and of the mind; and were by nature the children of wrath, even as others."

Praise God, Paul didn't stop there. Paul went on to say in the next two verses, "But God, who is rich in mercy, for his great love wherewith he loved us, even when we were dead in sins, hath quickened us together with Christ, (by His grace ye are saved)". Praise be unto God for that little phrase that we often overlook, "But God". That one phrase makes the difference between heaven and hell. "But God" who is rich in mercy. For the Holy Spirit came and removed the blinders from our eyes, and allowed the light of Jesus Christ to shine into our hearts and we are saved. And if it were not for the Holy Spirit removing the blinders from us we would be lost and separated from the Lord Jesus Christ forever.

We need to thank God "daily" for sending the Holy Spirit to our aid to help us fight the enemy that tries to use our minds as his playground. We need to "daily" invite the Holy Spirit to take control of our thought life and remove anything that is not of God. And guide us into a deeper relationship with the Father, the Son & the Holy Spirit. For we have the power through the Spirit in Jesus' name to rebuke the enemy out of our minds and the enemy will have to leave! You do not, and I repeat, you do not have to entertain the devil.

A desensitized mind can interfere with our thinking and hinder us from thinking godly and wholesome thoughts. {Eph.4:18-19} We can see through these passages of scripture how that people can lose all sensitivity, and how that they are no longer sensitive to the Holy Spirit. When people continually expose their minds to sin, violence, cruelty and negative thoughts they become conditioned by those elements, and are slowly desensitized by them. When we continually expose our minds to the things that are contrary to God's word and will for our lives we become insensitive to the convicting power of God's Spirit and our conscience is seared.

1 Tim.4:2 speaks of demon-inspired false teachers" whose consciences have been seared with a hot iron." This is exactly why we have to be very careful of everything we expose ourselves to, because every evil or immoral image that enters our mind tends to sear our conscience, and desensitized us to sin. We have an entire society whose conscience has been seared and desensitized by the filth and pollution of this world. We must not allow the enemy of this world to play with our minds and use us it as his playground in the area of our minds to the point that the devil has desensitized our minds to sin against the God. If you allow the enemy in your mind and you don't rebuke him out, he will have full rein in your thought life. Don't allow this to happen! You can find help through the power of Jesus Christ to resist the enemy and he has to flee at Jesus' name. Even the demons tremble at the very name of Jesus! Praise God! We have the victory in Jesus' wonderful name.

Also a depraved mind can interfere with our thinking and hinder us from thinking godly and wholesome thoughts. If our minds become darkened we can quickly become desensitized in our mind. And then the next step is for a person to develop a depraved {corrupt} mind. While many of the readers of this book my say "David, I don't commit the gross moral sins that the bible condemns". That really could be true, however, there are other sins that we commit that I believe are just as destructive as murder, adultery, fornication and a lot more sins that I could name. I know some of you will disagree with me but that's okay. I am obligated by the calling of God on my life to speak the truth. God's truth! There are some things that we as Christians do that fall into the same category as murder, fornication, adultery and wickedness.

Rom.1:29-30..." Being filled with all unrighteousness, fornication, wickedness, covetousness, maliciousness; full of envy, murder, debate, deceit, malignity; whisperers, Backbiters, haters of God, despiteful, proud, boasters, inventors of evil things, disobedient to parents." The NIV version says "they have become filled with every kind of wickedness, evil, greed and depravity. They are full of envy, murder, strife, deceit and malice. They are gossips, slanderers, God-haters, insolent, arrogant and boastful; they invent ways of doing evil; they disobey their parents". The New Living Translation says "Their lives become full of every kind of wickedness, sin, greed, hate, envy, murder, fighting, deception, malicious behavior, and gossip. They are backbiters, haters of God, insolent, proud, and boastful. They are forever inventing new ways of sinning and are disobedient to their parents".

"Whisperers" means revealer of secrets, talebearer. It comes from another word that means "to utter an untruth or attempt to deceive by falsehood". "Backbiter" means evil speaking of someone or to slander someone, to dishonor, belittle or give a bad name". Gossiping, backbiting and speaking evil of others with the intent to defame, damage or slander someone else name or reputation are sins that fall in the same category as murder! When we speak evil of others with the intent to defame or slander their name or reputation, in the eyes of God that's the same as murder. As Christians we need to guard our minds against such things as this. Titus.3:2 tells us that we should speak evil of no man. As Christians we need not to let the devil have our minds as his playground, because when the enemy starts playing with your mind and you allow him to, you are then setting yourself up for a serious fall in your walk in God!

In closing this chapter, the bible speaks of a double- mind. James.1:8 says a double-minded man is unstable in all his ways. You may say what is double-mind? It describes a person who continually goes back and forth between God's way of thinking and their own way of thinking. I told you previously, that we have only two basic ways of thinking and operating. You live according to facts and you live according to human reason. A double- minded person is one who is straddling the fence and playing both sides. A double- minded person expects God to forgive him or her of all their sins, but cannot find the capacity to forgive other people who have sinned against them. A double-minded person praises God on Sunday, then participates in unholy language of this world during the entire week. A double-minded person is an unreliable person who is unstable in ALL their ways.

Col.3:2 says…"Set your affections (mind) on things above, not on things on the earth". We as children of the Most High God need to set our minds on the things of God and don't let our self be distracted by the enemy in anyway shape or form. Don't become double-minded! What does it mean to set your mind on things above? It means to decide once and for all that you are not going to allow the devil to use your mind as his playground and not to listen to his lies that he is trying to place in your mind but to listen and to think God's way and live God's way. And be determine to focus on God and His plan for your life. Refuse to be deterred or distracted by any thing that the enemy may try to bring to you to contradict Christ and His control in our lives. Give no place to the devil in your thought life…. turn it ALL over to Jesus.

Chapter Four:
Choices.

The definition of the word "choice" is the act of choosing. There are two choices that we can make in our lives. One is the right choice and the other is the wrong choice. And it all starts with the right decisions that we make from our thinking, in our mind, and this is where the devil loves to make a playground is in the area of your decisions if you allow him to. Our choices reveal the kind of person we are, but also there is another side to it. We may, by our choices, also determine what kind of person we will become. Its all about making the right choices. We as Christians need to ask God for an awareness in our decision-making as well as a renewed commitment to make the right ones.

Choices--they are giving to us by God. We see in Gen.2:15-17 that God gave Adam responsibility for the garden and God told him not to eat from the tree of the knowledge of good and evil. Rather than physically preventing him from eating. God gave Adam the choice, and thus the possibility of choosing wrongly. And God also gives us choices every day, and we often choose wrongly. Because so many times we allow the devil to use our minds as his play ground and thus we make the wrong decisions and these wrong choices may bring pain, but if we will learn from these wrong choices, we will grow and make better choices in our future. Because living with the consequences of our choices teaches us to think and choose more wisely. So don't allow the enemy to use your mind as his playground and then you make the wrong choice because the enemy has placed that choice there.

You can make choices of disobedience and it becomes foolish. For in the book of Duet.11:26 it says," Behold I set before you this day a blessing and a curse". We see here where God set before the Israelites a choice… a choice between blessings and curses. And you know what they chose, the curse. And as Christians today we have that same choice. We can live for ourselves the enemy or live in service to God. But my Christian friends to choose our way is to travel on a dead-end road, but to choose God's way is to receive eternal life. For in the book of John.5:24 it says, "Verily, verily, I say unto you, He that heareth my word, and believeth on him that sent me, hath everlasting life, and shall not come into condemnation; but is passed from death unto life".

We as Christians need so very much to base all of our choices upon the word of God and through prayer. We will be able to run the devil out of our minds, and we will put up a sign letting the devil know that there is NO VACANSIES! in our thought life, and to pack up his play-ground and split. We must have a prayer life as well as studying the word of God in order to keep the devil on the run. But ultimately it's our choice! Which will you choose this day? A blessing or a curse?

Our choices and the effects should be considered all at one time. You can read in the book of Prov.1:10-19 that we must learn to make choices, not on the basis of flashy appeal or short-range pleasure, but in view of long-range effects. And sometimes this will mean steering clear of those people who want to entice us into activities that we know are wrong. You can't be friendly with sin and expect your life to remain unaffected. We can't allow the devil to set up a play-ground of sin in our minds and think that we won't be affected by it. For what goes into your mind will come out just as it went in… good or bad. So, my friends, think upon the things of our Lord Jesus Christ.

Choices… when made right they have great benefits. Prov.13:6…" Righteousness keepeth him that is upright in the way: but wickedness overthrows the sinner". My friend every choice for good sets into motion other opportunities for good. Each decision we make to obey God's word will bring a greater sense of order to our lives, but each decision we disobey from God's word will bring confusion and destruction. And, child of God, the right choices you make reflect your integrity, as well And obedience brings the greatest safety and security. Don't allow the devil to put up a play-ground of disobedience in your mind.

Matthew made the right choice to follow Jesus for salvation. Matt.9:9 says, " And Jesus passed forth thence, he saw a man, named Matthew, sitting at the receipt of custom: and he said unto him, 'Follow me'. And he arose and followed him." And at that time two changes happened in Matthew when he decided to follow Jesus. First of all, Jesus gave him a new life. Matthew not only belonged to a new group, he belonged to the Son of God. Matthew was not just accepting a different way of life, he was now an accepted person. For a despised tax collector, that change must have been wonderful! Second, Jesus gave Matthew a new purpose for his skills. When he followed Jesus, the only tool from his past job that he carried with him was his pen. From the beginning, God made him a record-keeper.

As children of God we made the right choice when we accepted Jesus Christ into our lives, and the only way to keep serving Jesus is not to allow the enemy to over take our minds with his play-grounds of sin. For we can resist the enemy and he will flee from us. Just put on the whole amour of God. Plug into the spiritual realm and think on the things of Christ. Plug into the spiritual realm and be His voice, hands, and feet. Because you may be the only Christ that people see. Don't allow the enemy to keep you going around in the wilderness of your mind and to keep you from your promise land of victory in the control of your mind through Christ Jesus. For the battle is not ours'... it belongs to the Lord.

Joseph made the right choice about the temptation of seduction. Gen.39:7-9... "And it came to pass after these things, that his master's wife cast her eyes upon Joseph, and she said, Lie with me. But he refused, and said unto his master's wife, Behold, my master wotteth {to know} not what is with me in the house, and he hath committed all that he hath to my hand. There is none greater in this house than I; neither hath he keep back any thing from me but thee, because thou art his wife: how then can I do this great wickedness, and sin against God?"

Saint of God, when the enemy comes to us in some other shape or form and tries to entice our mind with his play-ground of sin, be just like Joseph, be determined not to allow the devil to turn your victory into wickedness and sin against your God. For if you take a stand against the enemy that is trying to place his play-ground of sin into your mind, God will see you through to the victory and you will go higher with God than you have ever been. Take the time to give God the victory and praise over your mind right now as you read this. Stop reading this book for a minute and kneel down and pray. Thank God for the victory over your mind through Jesus Christ and then come back and read on for further wisdom.

Also Boaz made the right choice about his spouse. Lets look at Ruth's choice. Ruth.1:16-17...."And Ruth said Intreat me not to leave thee or to return from following after thee: for whither thou goest, I will go; and where thou lodgest, I will lodge: thy people shall be my people, and thy God my God: Where thou diest, I will die, and there will I be buried: the Lord do so to me, and more also, if ought but death part thee and me." Just look at her care and Boaz's compassion... there came a ceremony and wedding bells started ringing. See. my friend, it is by the right choices, you make that will determine our destiny and just how far we go with our Lord and Savior Jesus Christ. So don't allow the enemy to place his play-ground of sin into your mind and then you began to believe a lie that has been placed there by the enemy. For God will give you the victory to make the right choices in your life and the victory to win this battle of the mind.

Here is a little chart that will help you to make the right choices in all areas of your life. Just ask yourself these questions the next time you are to make a choice.

1.   Will this choice cause someone else to sin?
2.   Does this choice glorify God?
3.   Will this choice help me do my best?
4.   Is this choice against a specific command in the scripture and would thus cause me to sin?
5.   Will this choice help my witness for Christ?

Before you make a choice, ask "What would Jesus do?" We can defeat the enemy, but you must know how, and this is a start on how you can destroy the devil's play-ground of sin in your mind. Praise God for the victory! For help is on it's way.

Chapter Five:
It's Our Choice To Make Life Count

Let's look at a man in Hebrews 11:23-27 who made a great impact on the world just because he didn't allow the enemy to set up a play-ground of sin in his mind. Because he chose to make life count for something. He was just an ordinary man who accomplished extraordinary tasks because he chose to do certain things the right way. To do things God's way and not the enemy's way. We can discover how we can make our lives count through the right choices that we make and defeat the devil at his game. Life is made up of choices. You may be saying at this point that you had no choice in your birth, and to that point I will agree. However, how a person lives his or her life after they are born and grown is their choice.

Deut.30:19 says," I call heaven and earth to record this day against you, that I have set before you life and death, blessing and cursing: therefore choose life, that both thou and thy seed may live."

God is telling each of us that the life that we live is made up of choices…blessed ones or cursed ones. Don't allow the enemy to set up a play-ground of sin in your mind to the point that you don't receive Christ into your life. God says, "I have set before you life and death, blessing and cursing"… then he encourages us to choose life. How you and I live our lives as a Christian individual is our choice. Don't blame God for your messed up life. The way you live your life as a person is your choice.

My friend it is my heart's desire and my prayer that you will choose to live your life for God in such a way that it will impact those around you. The enemy is out to set up a play-ground in your mind to make you believe a lie and die and go to hell. Please…. don't allow this, for you can escape this place called hell and have life with King Jesus. Just ask Jesus to come into your heart, tell him that you are a sinner and to save you from your sins and Jesus will come in and you will be set free, from the play-ground of the devil's sin in your life. Praise God for the Victory!

Lets look at Moses, a man that had to make a choice concerning the direction and quality of his life. Because of his choice, he received the ten commandments from God. He lead the children of Israel out of 400 years of bondage and slavery in Egypt. Moses wrote the first five books of the Bible. Moses was a man that God used in an amazing way to accomplish an amazing task.

You and I as well can be used by God to do great and mighty things, if only we will listen to Him and follow His voice just as Moses did. Lets not allow the enemy to set up his play-ground in our minds and keep us back from what God has called us to do in this end time harvest. Because the devil would like to keep you and I back from accomplishing the amazing task and work that our God has set before us, and that is to preach and teach the word of God to all people, to see souls saved and added to the kingdom of God. We can walk in the victory over the battles of our minds and do just what God wants to get accomplished in the world through us.

Moses chose God and he made a number of very important choices about his life. Moses did not allow the enemy to set up play-grounds of sin in his mind and keep him back from what God wanted him to accomplish. He became one of the prominent people in the Bible. By the choices he made, Moses settled four key issues about his life and just who he was. Also we must settle these issues as well if our lives are going to count for anything. And we must not allow the devil to set up his play-ground in our minds and tell us anything different.

The four issues that Moses settled that you and I must settle as well are:

1. The issue of identity. Who am I in Christ?
2. The issue of responsibility. What am I going to do with my life for Jesus to make it count?
3. The issue of priority. What is really the most important thing in life that I can do for God? 4.The issue of difficulty. How much am I willing to commit to what I'm going to give my life for Jesus Christ?

These are issues that each one of us as Christians will have to deal with. Moses made the right choice in each instance.

Today, you and I as well can make the right choices, by resisting the devil out of our minds. Stop allowing him to set these play-grounds of defeat in our minds. Stop allowing him to tell you that you can't because you CAN do all things through Christ Jesus. Don't allow the enemy to win the battle of the mind, when we can have the mind of Christ. For you are a new man or a new woman in Jesus Christ. Get to the point in your life that you tell the devil there is NO VACANCY! here in my mind for you to even think that you can set up a play-ground here in the name of Jesus.

I would like to give you four foundations for personal success that the enemy would like for you not to know and for you not to receive in your life.

1. I have to discover what God made me to be.
2. I have to accept responsibility for my own life.
3. Establish a value system for my life.
4. Never take my eyes off the vision and goal that God has placed in my life. For people who succeed in their life are focused on the vision that God has placed there.

Discover what God made you to be. You are "someone" in God and don't let the enemy tell you anything different! Don't let him place his play-ground of doubt and fear in your mind and tell you that you are nothing when you are someone for God. You are a King's Kid with royal blood flowing through your veins, the blood of Jesus Christ. Tell the devil to pack up his toys and leave your mind, for Jesus lives here and you are covered by His blood.

Moses was born a Hebrew slave but he was raised as Pharaoh's grandson in Pharaoh's palace. Moses had an identity crisis big time! He had to decide: am I a Hebrew or am I Egyptian? Am I a slave or am I royalty? The major consequences of that decision would affect the rest of his life. If he chooses to say, "I'm Pharaoh's grandson he has fame, fortune, a life of luxury, a promising career, heir to the throne. And if he chose to say, "I'm a Hebrew and son of Hebrew slaves," he'll be rejected. He'll be despised. He'll be thrown out, humiliated and he'll live a life of a slave the rest of his life. Moses made the right choice because he refused to live a lie. He was a man of the utmost integrity and character.

Moses did NOT allow the enemy to set up a play-ground of sin in his mind and make him to believe a lie that he was an Egyptian. Instead, Moses took a stand for what he knew was best and that was that he was Hebrew. See, we can't allow the enemy to set up a play-ground of lies in our mind and tell us that we are something else when we know that we are not. We need to be men and woman of the utmost integrity. And tell the devil just who we are in Christ Jesus.

Moses made his decision in verse 24,"By faith, Moses, when he was come to years, refused to be called the son of Pharaoh's daughter." See "refused" here means to disown, reject, to leave no door open. It's settled and done. Moses insisted on being what God made him to be and no amount of peer pressure could convince him otherwise.

As Christians we should refuse, disown, reject, and leave no door open to our minds for the enemy to set up his play-ground, so that we will be able to make and do the right decisions and insist on being what God made us to be and no amount of pressure from the enemy could and would convince us otherwise. Because we didn't allow the enemy to set up his play-grounds of sin in our minds. Praise God for the victory that we have through Christ Jesus.

Acts.7:22-25..." And Moses was learned in all the wisdom of the Egyptians, and was mighty in words and in deeds. And when he was full forty years old it came into his heart to visit his brethren the children of Israel. And seeing one of them suffer wrong, he defended him, and avenged him that was oppressed, and smote the Egyptian: For he supposed his brethren would have understood how that God by his hand would deliver them: but they understood not."

Moses was a great man on his way to becoming the next Pharaoh of Egypt. But there came a time in his life that he would have to decide who he was going to be. Was he going to listen to the enemy or was he going to do the right thing by listening to God? Was he going to be an Egyptian or a Hebrew? See, the enemy could have been telling him "look you can be a Pharaoh," {setting up the play-ground in his mind} "you can rule Egypt" or "you could be a Hebrew and lead your people out of bondage"… which do you choose Moses? But do you know what Moses chose? He chose to be identified with his own people and gave up fame and power of Egypt. See, Moses knew that God had a plan and purpose for his life and he chose the life that God had for him.

Sometimes we will have to lose fame, prestige, and power to do the plan that God called us into. Don't allow the enemy to paint pictures in your mind of how it "could" be if you did it your way. Say "NO!" devil you won't set up this play-ground in my mind for me to lose out what

God has already placed here for my life. My friend, God has made you for His purpose. God has a plain for you already made out. He has a purpose for your life. He just wants you to be YOU and if you will not be you, who will you be?

The first secret of success is to be who you really are. The person God meant for you to be. Stop allowing the devil to set up his play-ground in your mind and tell you to be something or someone that you really aren't. That should relieve a lot of stomach ulcers, nervous disorders, migraines, etc., and bring you a lot of peace. Stop allowing the enemy to conform you to others, that's a play-ground. Stop allowing the devil to make you look like everybody else, drink like everybody else, talk like everybody else, and buy the same things everybody else has. These are all play-grounds that the devil will place in your mind if you allow him to. Just be yourself in God and discover what God made you to be. God made Moses to be a leader to a suffering people. Praise God for making you who you are today.

We need to accept responsibility for our own life. You need to stop making excuses and stop blaming others for your messed up life. You need to take the initiative. Stop allowing the enemy to set up play-grounds of excuses and of blaming others in your mind. Just look at what Moses did in verse 25, he chose to be mistreated along with the people of God rather than to enjoy the pleasures of sin for a short time. Choices! If you want to make an impact with your life, it's your choice. See, we can be as close to God as we want to be or as far away as we want to be. We can read the bible as much as we want or not. But it's YOUR CHOICE! God has given you the freedom of choice and the choices we make will determine our future. Don't allow the enemy to place the play-ground of wrong choices in your mind. But choose you this day whom you will serve.

We see in verse 24 where Moses was "refusing" and in verse 25 we have Moses "choosing." Moses follows a "negative" action with a "positive" action. In verse 23, God chose Moses as a baby, but in verse 25 Moses chose God. My friend, God may have chose you as a child and the enemy is placing all kinds of play-grounds of sin in your mind to keep you from choosing God. Please… don't allow this to take place any longer for you DO have a purpose in the kingdom of God! Tell the enemy that he has had your mind and soul much too long and to take his play-ground of toys and be gone in Jesus' name! Because this day you chose to serve the Lord and there is "NO VACANCY!" in your mind or life for him. And then give God the Praise for what He has done in your life and mind.

In verse 24.... "By faith Moses, when he had grown up." Look at that passage..."when Moses had grown up." Maturity is when people start accepting responsibility for their own actions and lives. It's maturity when people stop allowing the enemy to place a play-ground of blaming other people in our minds and start accepting responsibility for their own lives. See, as a baby it was okay for Moses to live off of his parent's faith in order to learn and grow. But when he had grown up, he had to make decisions on his own. He had to go God's way because he CHOSE to go God's way.

See, when we are first saved sometimes we live off of our friends or family's faith. But don't allow the enemy to place in your mind his play-ground to the point that you stay a "baby" in other people's faith to where you don't grow and start accepting your own faith and responsibility and make the right decisions based upon the things of God for your own life.

We can't live off of other people's spiritual commitments. I know you have heard people say, "My parents were Christians" or "My dad is a minister" or "My husband/wife is a believer". So what? You still YOU OWN personal relationship with God through Jesus Christ. Some Christians are still allowing the enemy to place his play-ground in their minds and they are at a stand still with God. Some still are spiritual babies.... it's time to grow up. You have got to stop living off the spiritual "apron strings" of your parents and friends in the Lord and get your own faith. When Moses grew up, he made a choice.

My friend, I can't blame others for the direction of my life, but the enemy says the opposite. He say's it's not your fault. You're the product of your environment. Blame other people for your messed up life. Did you know the way you look at the word "blame" it is B--LAME. When you began to blame you are being lame. You can't blame other people for the direction of your life. It's your life! Not another's. Let me just say here, you can't control all the circumstances but YOU CAN CHOOSE HOW YOU RESPOND. No one can ruin my life, not even the enemy, if I don't give in to his mind games. I am free to choose my response.

We need to establish a proper system of values for our life. If you are going to make life count you need to settle the issue of what is REALLY important. Clarify it in our lives. Moses did just that. He clarified his values and priorities. Do not allow the enemy to set up a play-ground in your mind to the point that you don't establish a proper system of values for your life, because the devil would have you messed up in your mind so that you would have no values in your life at all. Don't allow the devil to do this to you in your life.

In verse 26..." Esteeming the reproach of Christ greater riches than the treasures in Egypt: for he had respect unto the recompense of the reward." See, Moses regarded disgrace for the sake of Christ as greater value than the treasures of Egypt, because he was looking ahead to his reward. The word "regarded" means to evaluate, to consider, to weigh in the balances, to judge. It is not something that you do quickly. You need to sit down and seriously consider. What am I meant to live out in my life? What are you living for?

Moses evaluated what Egypt had to offer and then he evaluated what God had to offer. He evaluated the temporal pleasure of Egypt against the eternal blessing and pleasure of God and then chose to go with God. What Egypt had to offer was nothing compared to the glory of what God had to offer. You and I as Christians need to evaluate at times when there are things put into our minds, "Is this what the enemy has placed here to try and destroy me or is this what God has offered me?" And once we do this, if it is not of God, you can destroy that device that the devil is using as a play-ground in your mind and you will have the victory in Jesus name.

Most people have never done this and that's why they're failures at life and in their Christian walk with the Lord Jesus Christ. They don't know why they are, they don't know what they want to accomplish in life, and they don't know what's really important, because the enemy has a play-ground in there mind and he is using this as a tool to keep you from the blessings of God for your life. And the enemy is keeping them from establishing values in their life. The things that you would build your life on. The things that will be important to you and to God. Don't let it happen.

My friend, the fact is, if you don't decide what is important in your life through Jesus Christ, the enemy will place a play-ground there for you and you will give in to that mind game that he has placed there. You have got to make the right choices in your life or your life will ultimately be full of the results from the wrong choices you made. Rely upon Jesus!

The enemy is more than happy to pressure you and set up his playground in your mind if you allow him to. And to mold and promote his value system on you. We have a lot of Christians today who know the Lord, but they are bought into the enemies value system because they have allowed the enemy to set up a play-ground in their minds. And they are living out that system without even thinking about it rationally. They have automatically adopted it.

Just what is the enemy's value system?

1. Power and prestige. "I want to be famous". That is a play-ground for the enemy to use in your mind and life if you do it for the wrong reasons.
2. Pleasure. "I want to feel good. I want to be happy. I want to have fun." This is another play-ground that the enemy will place in your mind.
3. Possessions. "I want to make a fortune. I want to be wealthy." Another play-ground for the enemy to set up in your mind and life.

But, look my friend, if you would use these things for the good they really could be blessings from God above for your life. For if you have these things and you are not using them for God, then you must be using them for no good. And that is just what the enemy wants you to do, so rebuke him and set him straight and use the gifts that God gives you for the good. And you will be blessed coming in and going out. Praise God for victory!

But what's ironic is that Moses, by the world's standard, had it made. He had all the above:

1: Power. He was heir to the throne of the most powerful country of the world at that time.
2: Pleasure. Every whim would be satisfied in the palace of Egypt. He was on easy street so to speak.
3: Possessions. The wealth of the world was concentrated in Egypt.

Moses had it all. Power, Pleasure, Possessions. Moses had it all but he got up and walked away from it all. The very three things most of us spend our lives trying to accomplish. Why? Because he knew that it would not last. See Moses seen ahead and he knew the enemy and the world's values won't last. See Moses was not allowing the enemy to set up any play-grounds in his mind that could be used against him in any way. Moses said "yes" to God and His way of thinking.

You must realize that when you say "Yes" to God, you are removing the play-grounds that the enemy has been setting up in your mind. Because when you say "yes" to God it means "No" to the enemy. My friend, it is so easy to say "Yes" to God than to let the enemy have his way in your life and in your mind. A lot of people want Christ, plus all the things that the devil has placed in their minds as well. Come Sunday they put God on like some garment and have a little time for Him. But really they are buying into the enemy's system that he has placed in their mind. But, you see, Jesus said in God's Word... "You can't serve two masters." The problem with a lot of Christians today is that they are afraid to say "No" to the enemy's play-ground of the mind.

What you lose when you don't say "No" to the enemy and his mind games: you lose your happiness. Your happiness becomes compromised and it only makes you miserable when you try to live for the Lord and listen to the enemy. This can't be done. It will make you miserable. You need to learn how to say "NO" to the enemy who is trying to set you up. And you need to learn to say it with conviction and power in authority. I am not going to be sucked up into the enemy's play-ground in my mind. That rat race, the empty lifestyle that says life consists of carnal pleasures and passions... they just doesn't last. Moses stood his ground in fight for his mind. You can as well.

Just what was Moses' value system? There was three things that had value to Moses. He discovered that God's purpose was more valuable than popularity. Don't allow the enemy to place a play-ground of popularity in your mind and make you think that it is more valuable than God's purpose. Moses knew that God had a plan for his life....'I am going to lead the Israelites to freedom as God has told me to do.' He refused to be called the son of Pharaoh's daughter.

People are more valuable than pleasures. In verse 25.... Moses chose to be mistreated along with the people of God (they were in slavery at the time) rather than enjoy the pleasures of sin for a season. Do not allow the enemy to fooling you with his play-ground of sin to the point that we fall into sin and think that it is a pleasure, when it is just for a short time and then you will pay for your sins and be separated from Jesus Christ. I like that verse. The Bible always tells the truth. The Bible never lies or sugar-coats the truth. Praise God!

That says there is pleasure in sin. The Bible says sin is fun. If it were a bummer no one would do it. BUT it is just for a short time! It does not last! Moses could have temporary pleasure being the next Pharaoh of Egypt or he could go do what God had called him to do and help the people who were in pain, who needed to be set free. But Moses did not give into the play-ground of the enemy. He could have stayed there in the pleasure and today no one would even have known the name of " Moses". He would just be some decomposed mummy in the Pharaoh's tomb in Egypt. No one would have known him as a deliverer for God and His people. But Moses chose the right thing, and you and I today must choose the right thing. Will it be the play-grounds of sin that the devil places in our mind or will it be the things of God that He tells us in our mind to do? It's our choice. Choose you this day whom you will serve.

My friends, God's peace is more valuable than possessions... verse 26..."Moses regarded the disgrace for the sake of the Lord as of greater value than the treasures of Egypt." And in verse 24, Moses rejects the world's measure of success. And in verse 25, he rejects the world's pleasure. And in verse 26, he rejects the world's treasure. Moses chose to do what was right in his mind and not what the enemy would have liked for him to choose to do. Moses knew that God's peace is more important than possessions. He could have stayed in the palace of Egypt and had what ever he wanted---wine, women, and song. But, you see, Moses knew that no possession that the enemy might try and set up for him, could ever give him that inner peace in God.

Moses would have been the most miserable person by not listen to God and what God wanted him to do. But Moses chose not to let the enemy set up any kind of play-ground in his mind to keep him from doing the work that God wanted him to do. You and I must not allow the enemy to set up any kind of play-ground that will keep us from doing the things that God has called us to do. Let me say, peace does not come from the things you own in this life, peace comes from being in the center of God's will, being what God made you to be, doing what God made you to do, this is where peace comes from. Not from the play-grounds of sin that the enemy places within your mind but from what God places in your mind to do and you do them for God.

What do you value? What matters most?

The issue is that the peace of God in your mind is far more better than the play-grounds of sin that the enemy tries to place there. That's what counts with God and that should be what counts with us as Christians. Does it amaze you that Moses gave up the very things that a lot of people spend their lives trying to get? What, may you say, motivated this man named Moses? What made him do that and live that way? Because he was looking ahead to his rewards in God!

Moses had a right perspective. He did not allow the enemy to set up play-grounds of the world in his mind. What motivates you to not reject what the enemy is trying to place in your mind? It's your perspective. It's all in what you're looking at. Are you looking at the "here and now" with disregard toward your heavenly reward? See, Moses looked beyond this life into the next life. The life we live here is to prepare us for the life that we will live in heaven with our God. You and I need to look beyond this life and look into the here after. Don't allow the enemy to deceive you and play games with your mind to the point that you don't know who you are in Jesus Christ. For you are a King's Kid, a child of the Most High God and we have the victory in Christ Jesus over the play-grounds that the enemy tries to set up in our minds. Give God the praise at this time for you are not defeated! For Jesus is Lord!

Your values are determined by your visions. Don't ever lose the visions that God has placed in you. For the enemy would love to place the play-ground of doubt and fear in your mind to the point that you do not go for that vision or visions that the Lord Jesus Christ has placed there. Whatever you are looking at is what becomes most important in your life. What kind of pictures do you have within your mind? Are they of God or are they what the enemy has placed there? What is most important in your life? Do you fill your mind with the Bible… God's holy word? What are you focusing on? What are you looking at? What is the most important thing to you? See, Moses was a man of vision. He had his faith in God.

Let's never allow the enemy to place his play-grounds of sin in our minds…we will loose focus of God and our goals for Him. Verse 27…. "By faith he forsook Egypt, not fearing the wrath of the king: for he endured, as seeing him who is invisible." You must stay focused on God and his purpose for your life and not allow the enemy to place doubt and fear within your mind… "for we can do ALL things through Christ Jesus that strengthens me,"…… we have the victory!! People that want there lives to count, they are people who will stay focused on what God wants them to do. You will constantly keep it before you. Why is vision so important? The secret of success is persistence. The secret of persistence is vision. Vision draws you on so that when you want to give up… you don't. You have your eyes on the ultimate reward. You don't give in and you don't give up….ever!

The enemy would love to place a play-ground of doubt and fear in your mind so that you would just give up on the vision and not stay focused on what God has placed in you. We MUST persevere. This is the key to foundational success for Moses… he had tremendous endurance. He refused to give up no matter what happened--- impossible situations, critics, whatever. You see Moses spent most of his life waiting. From the time that God gave Moses the vision, the dream of setting free the entire nation of Israel after 400 years of bondage and slavery to the time it was fulfilled and ready to go into the Promised Land was 80 years.

How about you? Could you wait that long and not give into the devil's play-ground of the mind? The devil would like for you to give in and give up on the vision He has showed you. If God tells you something and it doesn't happen until 80 years later, will you stay focused? See, Moses spent 40 years in Midian just waiting for God to say, "Okay, let's get started." Let me ask you this--- Do you ever get tired of waiting on God? If you do, the devil has placed a play-ground there to get you to give up. But hold on… for the miracle is in the making. Don't give up and don't give into the games of the enemy. Do delays ever tempt you to give up? Have you learned the difference between "No" and "Not just yet?" Have you learned that God's delays are not necessarily denials, as the enemy would have you to believe? One of the tests of our faith is just how long can you wait upon God? For you and I must keep our eyes upon the vision that God has placed upon us and not allow the enemy to set up his play-ground of doubt and fear in our minds.

Hebrews 12:1-2 says, "Wherefore seeing we also are compassed about with so great a cloud of witnesses, let us lay aside every weight, and the sin which doth so easily beset us, and let us run with patience the race that is set before us. Looking unto Jesus the author and the finisher of our faith; who for the joy that was set before him endured the cross, despising the shame, and is set down at the right hand of the throne of God."

My friends, let us run with patience and let's fix our eyes upon Jesus----those two go together. For when you and I fix our eyes upon Jesus, we will run the race with patience. What have you got your eyes and mind upon? How many of these play-grounds have you settled in your life that the enemy has placed there? Have you settled the issues of identity of just who you are in Jesus Christ? So that you don't have to keep trying to dress and act and be like everybody else in order to be accepted. Have you figured out the issue of responsibility? Have you said, I'm not going to blame anybody else for where I am or who I am?" For you are just as spiritual as you want to be. You can't blame anybody else. You're as committed as you want to be. And are you going to keep your eyes and mind upon God and the rewards that He has for you? Or are you going to allow the enemy to us your mind as his play-ground? It's your choice to make life count.

The most important issue is the relationship that you have with the heavenly Father God and Jesus. And if you haven't ever established a relationship with God because of the enemy's play-grounds of sin that he has placed in your life you can do so this day. Why wait? I don't understand why people would put off the most important thing in their life they will ever do. Say "yes" to Jesus and "No" to the enemy that has been playing with your mind for so long. Tell God "you have made me for a purpose" and "I want to start living in that purpose today." "I want to listen to You God and not the enemy" and "I want to go Your way God and accept Your values as my own... not the devil's". The choice is yours!! I pray that you make the right one in Jesus' name. Will you do it today? Then just praise God for the victory of your mind from the devil's grip.

Chapter Six:
We Must Stay Focused

Mark 8:22-25.... "And he cometh to Bethsaida; and they bring a blind man unto him, and he besought him to touch him. And he took the blind man by the hand, and led him out of the town; and when he had spit on his eyes, and put his hands upon him, he asked him if he saw ought. And he looked up, and said, I see men as trees, walking. After that he put his hands again upon his eyes, and made him look up: and he was restored, and saw every man clearly."

This is the only time in the word that Jesus touched someone twice. While this is the proper interpretation of the spiritual indictment against the blindness of Israel there is some applications for us. For we need not the enemy to set up a play-ground of spiritual blindness in our minds to the point that we can't receive what Christ has for us. For you and I must stay focused upon Christ. For it was the Lord and Savior Jesus Christ that touched the blind man and gave him his sight.

My friend, can you remember that day when Jesus touched you and opened up your blinded eyes and you saw light for the first time? For it flooded your darkened soul and took away the play-grounds of sin that the enemy had placed there. Christ enlightened your mind and you could see and understand clearly. When the enemy places play-grounds of sin in your mind you can't understand clearly. That is why we as Christians need to take control of our minds through Jesus Christ... the Son of the Living God. It's nice to know that as sinners lost and undone, we could come to know what Jesus could do for us. Jesus would forgive us of our sins and we would become His child. Do you remember that day?

Jesus touched this man and ask him, "What do you see?" This man replied, "I see men as trees walking ." He was not in focus yet. He was allowing the enemy to place a play-ground within his mind to the point that Jesus had to touch him twice and then he saw clearly. There was a time when Jesus touched you, opened your blinded eyes and you could see spiritual things. If you are not careful, the enemy will set up a play-ground in your mind again, so that you will not stay focused on the calling that God has placed within you. Don't allow this to take root in your life.

There are so many distractions in life. The devil would love to place in your mind these distractions so that you will keep your eyes off of Jesus and on to the things of this world and keep you from finishing the race and staying focused. If it gets to the place in your life where Jesus Christ can not be clearly seen, then everything else becomes blurred. Nothing will be in proper perspective in your life and your life will be totally out of focus. There are so many things that can get you out of focus. That is just where the enemy would love for you to stay…out of focus… taking a ride on his play-ground to defeat you in all areas of your mind and life. But you and I have the choice…..allow the enemy to set up his play-ground of sin in our minds or not. It's up to us!

Also the enemy can use people, problems, pressures and pain to can distract you. And if you will allow the enemy to use hypocrites, gossipers, trouble makers, and someone that you know that is putting on an act, to the point that you get your eyes off of Jesus and your attention upon these things, then the enemy has set up a play-ground within your mind. At times you don't even know why things are going so bad in your spiritual life. Could it be that you have allowed it to happen to you and that it just has not been revealed to you at this point? Well, my friend, you can have the victory over this problem in your mind that the enemy has placed there. Just give it to Jesus and then thank Him for the victory over it.

People who are distractions to some Christian's walk in the Lord cause them to say, "I see them in the choir," "I see them in Sunday school," and these people who are distracting them can cause them to get their eyes on the person and not Jesus. And that is just what the enemy wants to place in your mind just one of his play-ground toys so that you will not stay focus on what God has called you to do. And then all of a sudden your whole life is out of focus and you began to look at the play-ground of toys that the enemy has placed there within your mind. My friends, get your eyes off of the distractions Satan has placed there in your life and get your eyes on the Son of God...Jesus Christ. Be careful of this play-ground that the enemy sets up! He will get your mind on people so you won't stay focused upon the work of God. Get your vision cleared and see the Savior one more time!

Hebrews.12:2 says, "Looking unto Jesus the author and the finisher of our faith: who for the joy that was set before him endured the cross, despising the shame, and is set down at the right hand of the throne of God."

Child of God, the only way for us to live straight is for you and I to keep our eyes upon the lovely Lord Jesus Christ and not allow the enemy to use our mind as his play-ground at anytime!!! Don't allow the enemy to place in our minds to see people and problems {circumstances}, but for us to see God and His Son Jesus Christ only!!! You may say, "That sounds good preacher and I am in agreement but how do I do that?" How? Matthew.22:37 says, "Jesus said unto him, Thou shalt love the Lord thy God with all thy heart, and with all thy soul, and with all thy mind."

If someone asked you, "Do you love the Lord?" You say, "Yes, I love Him with all my heart." What about all your mind? My friend, that means you pull all your thought life into focus and you love Jesus through your thoughts as well. You love Jesus in your mind, for if you love Jesus with all your mind, then you will be able to stay focused.

Every God called preacher in this world today knows just how hard it can be at times in their ministry to stay focused when they are preaching. At times it's hard to stay focused when you having to look at some of their congregation yawning and looking at their watches. Every preacher knows the spiritual and mental warfare that goes on while they're preaching. It takes an enormous amount of focus to preach one sermon to one congregation. That is why, when the preacher goes home, he/she is totally exhausted. It took everything he/she had to get it done. But you see the preacher MUST stay focused. When the preacher is holding the congregation in attention and being intense in his/her presentation it is just like driving his/her car on ice. You have to stay focused or you could wreck badly!.

Don't allow the enemy to keep your head down when the man/woman of God is preaching.... delivering a message from God our Heavenly Father. You NEED to listen to what God has placed upon the heart of the messenger of God. You NEED to listen to what they are saying! A lot of prayers and tears have gone into the message that God has given them. See, the enemy would like to keep you from receiving what God has given to the messenger of God by placing his play-ground of thoughts into your mind to distract you in any kind of way that he possibly can. These distractions could overtake your mind if you don't learn to discipline yourself and stay focused on Jesus and what that He has for you to hear and do.

My friends, if you don't stay focused you will become distracted by people, problems, pressures and pain {circumstances} that you could have had the victory over. You will live a life of distractions and you will miss the blessings, the joy and the close walk that you could have had with Jesus and God the Father. When we stay focused on Jesus Christ, instead of our circumstances, our hearts will stay soft and warm and our heads will stay cool and our lives will be in order. If we can't see Jesus everything else becomes blurred to us. Don't allow the enemy to place his play-ground of distractions into your mind to get your focus off of Jesus and on to the distractions he has placed before you. Don't look to anything else....look to Jesus! Please stay focused on the Savior.

And there is another area that the enemy would like for you not to stay focused on...... and that is the Church....the body of Jesus Christ! As Christians we MUST stay focused on the Church as well. Let me explain..... because I know a lot of flags are going up here. We MUST see the Church as our Lord sees it. Just how important is the Church in the economy of God? Ephesians.5:25 says, "Husbands, love your wives, even as Christ also loved the church, and gave himself for it." You see, Christ gave His life for the church and that makes the Church of the upmost importance. We are commanded to be faithful to her, love her, and give to her.

We need men and women today that will preach the true word of God in our Churches so to see people born again and baptized in the Holy Ghost and with fire! Getting out the gospel of our Lord Jesus Christ. The churches today need old fashioned preaching desperately!!! The church services should be Spirit filled. The churches should have a strong witnessing program... winning souls for Christ. There must be strong fellowship among the saints so they can be able to reach out to the community through visitation and reaching the world through missions. Saints, we cannot allow the enemy to place his play-ground into our minds that we will just give up on what God has called us to do. WE MUST NOT LET UP!!!!

We must keep on having old fashioned Spirit filled gospel preaching, Spirit filled healing services, seeing people healed, seeing the people that have demonic spirits delivered and set free. Preachers and teachers of God the zeal must stay the same. Stay on fire the same as it was from the beginning through fasting and prayer. Don't allow the enemy to place play-grounds in your mind or ministry to the point that you please what man wants you to preach or teach. But preach what God has called you to preach and that is the true word of God from Genesis to Revelation and not to compromise the word of God for NO ONE!!! When our churches begin we want to see souls saved, the pews filled, to reach out into the community and to the world, to make a difference. Then we allow the distractions of the devil to get us sidetracked from what the real goal is. So we must stay focused on what God has called us to do and not allow the enemy to play with our minds. Stay focused on the Church as well.

You may say, "Well, I know what you're talking about, but I am getting older. Let the young ones have at it now." That is a lie from the enemy! 1 Peter.5: 1-2 says, "The elders which are among you, I exhort, who am also an elder, and a witness of the suffering of Christ, and also a partaker of the glory that shall be revealed: Feed the flock of God which is among you, taking the oversight thereof, not by constraint, but willingly; not for filthy lucre, but of a ready mind." It is the older generation's responsibility to work with the younger generation, teaching them what God has revealed unto you in your years of experience in service to Him. We NEED to work together! For it is about preaching and spreading the gospel of our Lord and Savior Jesus Christ to the younger souls as they come up in the Lord as well. Remember, who will take the older generation's place in the leading of souls to Jesus Christ, if we don't teach the younger generation of Christians to take our place? Don't allow the enemy to place a play-ground into your mind that you don't preach and teach what God has called you to do in these last days that we are living in.

Stop allowing the enemy to keep you from staying focused on the conclusion of your life! This is just what he would like to set up in your mind. For in the book of Acts.14:22 it says, "Confirming the souls of the disciples, and exhorting them to continue in the faith, and that we must through much tribulation enter into the kingdom of God." Everyone will finish this journey of our lives! BUT the true question is, "will you finish well?" Will you finish right, with honor, and with dignity? Will you die properly? We need so very much to stay focused on the conclusion of our life as well, Saints.

There are many believers that are no longer in the ministry…. they lost their focus. They got their eyes off of Jesus and began to look at the areas that the enemy placed into their minds. We NEED to stay focused on the Christian life and the things that God has placed within us or else we will not finish well. Don't allow the enemy to put you into a situation that may cause your testimony to be questioned or totally destroyed. So many believers fall into this trap! They allow the enemy to place his play-ground into their minds and they get caught up in the world and get their eyes off of Jesus and the work that He has called them into. We must finish right and well! Hebrews 12:1 says, "Wherefore seeing we also are compassed about with so great a cloud of witnesses, let us lay aside every weight, and sin which so easily besets us and let us run with patience the race that is set before us."

The "cloud of witnesses" are the children of God that have already gone on before us. They have finished their race and are now with God. And, my friends, if they could communicate with us they would surely say, "keep on going, keep the faith, because it will be worth it all at the finish line." We must trust God to take care of us. We must let Him take care of the cares of this world and keep our eyes on Him. The "finish line" is not a place. The "finish line" is a person and that person is Jesus Christ. My friends, stay focused on finishing this race. Keep your eyes on Jesus! And when the race is over you will hear Him say, "You stayed with it, you have did great, and now you are here with me, safe and across the finish line. Well done!" My friends, stay focused for His honor and glory.

Don't allow the enemy to use your mind as his play-ground to keep you back from anything that God has for you. Understand? Take back{!!!!} what the enemy is trying to steal from you. For you have the victory in Christ Jesus over the power of the enemy in your mind! Begin to give God the praise right now where you are!

Chapter Seven:
God Has A Formula For Great Success In Your Life

Joshua 1:1-11 (NIV), "After the death of Moses the servant of the Lord, the Lord said to Joshua the son of Nun, Moses' aid: Moses my servant is dead. Now then, you and all these people, get ready to cross the Jordan River into the land I am about to give to them----to the Israelites. I will give you every place where you set your foot, as I promised Moses Your territory will extend from the desert to Lebanon, and from the great river, the Euphrates----all the Hittite country----to the Great Sea on the west. No one will be able to stand up against you all the days of your life. As I was with Moses, so I will be with you; I will never leave you nor forsake you."

Verse 6.... "Be strong and courageous, because you will lead these people to inherit the land I swore to their forefathers to give them." Verse 7.... "Be strong and very courageous. Be careful to obey all the law my servant Moses gave you; do not turn from it to the right or to the left, that you may be successful wherever you go." Verse 8.... "Do not let this Book of the Law depart from your mouth; meditate on it day and night, so that you may be careful to do everything written in it. Then you will be prosperous and successful." Verse 9.... "Have I not commanded you? Be strong and courageous. Do not be terrified; do not be discouraged, for the Lord your God will be with you wherever you go."

Verse 10.... "So Joshua ordered the officers of the people: Verse 11.... "Go through the camp and tell the people, Get your supplies ready. Three days from now you will cross the Jordan here to go in and take possession of the land the Lord your God is giving you for your own (NIV)."

There was once a great man by the name of General Douglas MacArthur who said, "Joshua was one of the greatest generals who ever lived. The thing I like about Joshua is that he accomplished the impossible in spite of incredible odds and opposition. His life was one entire battle----one battle after another." Many of you who are reading this book can identify with that. Yet Joshua never gave up! We MUST NOT allow the enemy to set up a play-ground in our minds to the point that we give up in the heat of the battle. The word of God tells us that the battle is not ours', it belongs to the Lord! Praise the Lord! We don't have to give in to the devil's play-ground of the mind. We can have the victory over this area! Glory be to God!

We see that Joshua and the children of Israel are standing on the banks of the Jordan River. And on the other side of the Jordan lies their future. They are on the verge of crossing into the Promised Land. They have spent 40 years in the wilderness. Now they have come up, ready to cross the Jordan River, knowing that they are going to possess the promised land. God says in Joshua 1:11, "Three days from now you will cross the Jordan to go in and take possession of the land the Lord is giving you for your own." God said, "Joshua, you have a tremendous future ahead of you." God was telling Joshua, "I am going to do some great things in your life, and I will do everything I promised and more, IF you will listen to me and not the enemy of your mind. But it will be a fight; it's going to be a battle." Then God says, "You must take possession of what I want to give you."

God is trying to tell Christians that we have a tremendous future ahead of us! That we must take possession of what He has for us and not to allow the devil to set up play-grounds of doubt and fear into our minds so that we will not take possession of what God wants to give us. Don't allow the enemy to steal and rob you of the blessings that God wants to give you. You may be wondering just what does the future hold for you? Let me say, the answer to that is it's going to be a mixture of blessings and battles. But God is saying to you that He has great things that He wants to do in your life IF you will allow Him to fight for you! God has things for you that you haven't even thought of! He wants so much to bless you . The best days of our lives are ahead of us. But it will be a battle. You must be willing to and determined to lay hold of and possess your future! Don't allow the enemy to play with your mind to the point that you miss out on the blessings of God.

You maybe asking within yourself, "Pastor Love, how do I do that? Just how do I possess my future?" By doing the same three things that God told Joshua to do. In Joshua 1, God gives Joshua a good talking to. He says, "I know you're going to battle for the next 20 years so I want to encourage you." So, if you would try these three things, they will sustain you through life. If you will only do these three things, it will make an impact on your life. Twice in this chapter the word "success" is used. God was saying, "If you do these three things and don't allow the enemy to set up a play-ground in your mind of doubt, I will guarantee you "success" in life." It's God's strategy for our success. It's His strategy for possessing your future.

These three steps are as follows:

1. Set up a plan.
2. Stay in the Word.
3. Step out in faith.

God says, if you will do them, you can possess your future. We must take hold of it and not allow the enemy to set up any play-grounds in our minds to keep us back from this three step plan that God has for us.

Number 1: Set Up A Plan.

God tells us that we have got to plan for the future. But it has to be God's plan for our life. For God does have plans for your life. If you and I want to be more like God's child, we have got to learn how to plan. You need to plan for your future… for that is where you will spend the rest of your life. If you don't plan for it, the enemy will plan it for you, and we don't need that to take place in your life.

Joshua.1:2-3 (NIV) says, "Moses my servant is dead. Now then, you and all the people get ready to cross the Jordan River. I will give you every place where you set your foot, as I promised Moses." God says you and I must get ready for the future! We must prepare for the future! We must prepare to possess what God has promised .

We can see Joshua's response in verse 11(a), "So Joshua ordered the people, Get your supplies." Child of God, the future belongs to the ones who prepare for it. You MUST to have a plan and it MUST be God's plan and not the enemy's that he tries to place into your mind. We must stop the enemy before he even puts up the first sign of a play-ground because once he places a play-ground sign up in your mind he takes out the "G" in the sign and sets up "Sin." But we have the victory in our Lord Jesus Christ…. give Him the praise and glory!!!

My friends, success in life does not just happen! You just don't wake up one day and find out that you have become successful. It takes planning, on your part and my part. It takes work, it takes energy and it takes time. If you and I are going to succeed in our life for God and if we are going to make a really positive difference in our world for the glory of God, we must prepare with a plan. We must not allow the enemy to place his play-ground into our minds to get us off of the plan that King Jesus has for our lives. The enemy would like so very much for us to get our eyes and mind off of the things of God.

Dear Christian, have you started making plans? Don't just drift through life waiting for something wonderful to happen. Do you want to be a successful Christian? Then, my friend, plan to make your life count for God. Don't go through life without a purpose, a dream or a vision! Look at where you are going as a Christian and set up a plan to get you there where God wants you and do this planning with God! Don't leave God out of the planning! Don't allow the enemy to make you believe otherwise! For you can't plan your future without God in it all the way!

Joshua.1:2.... "Moses my servant, is dead." My friends, one of the ways you prepare yourself for the future is that you have to let go of the past. See, Joshua indeed was very close to Moses. Joshua had been with Moses for 80 years. He had been his understudy. But now Moses was a dead man. How would you like to have replaced Moses as leader? I am sure Joshua felt a bit nervous about that. Yet God was telling Joshua that He had a plan for his life. Sometimes in our lives we let past relationships keep us from possessing what God has for us in the future. It could be a death, someone hurting us, a divorce, a friend moves away, etc.. Just maybe you are saying, "How can I gain the approval of that person from my past?" While God is saying, "Let go of the past so that you can get on with the present." God just wants to work in your life and do great things through you and for you. So don't allow the enemy to set up play-grounds in your mind from the past. They can ruin your future in God.

Some of those who are reading this book for the first time are still hanging on to relationships that are absolutely no good for you and your walk with God. You are trying to prove yourself to people to whom you don't even need to prove yourself to. God said.... "Moses is dead! It's over. He's buried." Moses was dead but God wasn't!!! For God had a plan for a man named Joshua that went beyond what Moses had done. God said.... "You have to let go of these past relationships that have influenced you. Many were good and some were bad.... but just "let go and let God." We must learn that we have to bury our past or our past will bury us! "Let it go" and "let God" take control of it all! Joshua had to prepare himself and his future in God.

Child of God, the first key to knowing how to possess your future is set up a plan. Evaluate yourself. If you were asked to describe this very day in one word OR summarize your plans for the next year, what would it be my friend? Do you have a plan from God for your spiritual success OR is the enemy playing mind games with you to the point that you have missed out on the flow of the blessings that God had {and has} for your life?

Number 2: We must stay in the Word.

God was saying to Joshua, "You are going to be in battle for the next 25 years, and My Word is your instruction manual for conflicts. It is the manual for the battles of your life." Don't allow the enemy to place in your mind that you don't have to read the word of God daily. You and I will need to be instructed on how to gain ground in the midst of life's conflicts. For the word of God is our manual to fight the battles of the enemy's that come up against us in our mind or in any other way.

Verse7 (NIV)… "Be careful to obey all the Law. Do not turn from it to the right or the left that you may be successful wherever you go." God is saying in this verse… "Don't allow the enemy to get you sidetracked." Have you noticed how easy it is for some Christians to get sidetracked? To get off into other things that just aren't important? Areas that just doesn't really matter and are trivial?

Have you ever seen people come into the church, they are on fire for God, really excited, they give their lives to Christ, start out great and then get sidetracked? They get sidetracked by their career, sports, a hobby, having more children, etc. Somehow they lose focus off of Jesus and off the word of God. These are all play-grounds that the enemy will use in our mind and life.… IF we allow him to do so. Don't get me wrong, you can have these things in your life.… BUT IF they are becoming a "god" to you, to the point that you don't read and study God's word, stay on fire for God and his purpose your life, then they are taking the place of God the Father in your heart, mind and day to day life. The enemy has set up a play ground in your mind and life.

Child of God if we don't stay in the word of God we will get sidetracked. And other things will began to take priority over our spiritual life and spiritual growth in the Lord. And this is a play-ground that the enemy would love to set up in our minds and in our lives so that we will not grow with the Lord. You and I must stay in the word each and every day in order to fight the enemy in our minds. There are a lot of Christians that feed their stomachs three hot meals a day and maybe feed their spirits one cold snack a week. And then they wonder why they can't succeed in their Christian walk with God.

Joshua 1:8 says (NIV)…."Do not let this Book of the Law depart from your mouth, meditate on it day and night, so that may be careful to do everything written in it. Then you will be prosperous and successful."

We can see in verse 7 & 8 "success" is promised twice. God says, "Don't turn to the right or the left." Stay with the word of God, stay with the Book of the Law… you will be successful! God is saying to keep our minds saturated with the word of God and the things of God and you will be successful. God's promise of success has absolutely nothing to do with our own abilities. But God's promise of spiritual success in our lives has everything to do with "our commitment" to his Word. In fact, our ability to succeed in life comes as a result of our commitment to God's word. You may ask, "What do you mean by that?" Well, let me say this, as you stay committed to the word of God, His word will "develop in us" the ability to succeed. There will be no success in our Christian lives without God's word being active in it.

Can't you see why the enemy would love to place a play-ground in your mind and tell you that you don't have to study the word of God? If the enemy can do this he knows that he can keep you from being successful in your Christian walk with the Lord. You must guard your mind with the word of God so that the enemy will not distract you from what the Lord has planned for your life.

There are three ways that you can "stay in the word of God:"

1. Be careful to do everything written in it. Live the word of God. Be sure to always obey it.
2. Don't let it depart out of your mouth.. Discuss it with others. Talk about the Word of God.
3. Meditate on it day and night. Think on the word of God always.

If you do those things, God says that you will then become prosperous and successful. Think about the Word, talk about the Word, live the Word and watch God start blessing your life in a mighty way. It just don't apply to Joshua…. it also applies to your life and my life today..

2 Timothy 3:16 (Living Bible)… "The whole Bible was given to us by inspiration from God and is useful to teach us what is true and to make us realize what is wrong in our lives. It straightens us out and

helps us to do what is right." God's word "straightens me out," it shows me the path I walk on, how to walk on it. It shows me when I get off the path, how to get back on the path. It's good for doctrine, reproof, correction, instruction in righteousness that the man/woman of God may be thoroughly furnished unto every good work."

The Bible is our "Soul Food." Spurgeon once said… "a Bible which is coming apart is usually owned by someone who's not." Either your Bible is coming apart OR you are. It's your choice not to allow the enemy to play mind games with you, so that you don't grow spiritually with the Lord and stay in his word.

We can see in the word that Joshua was a busy man. He was a leader of an entire nation. He didn't have a whole lot of time. But he made the time to meditate on the word and to pray. He was a man of communion with God. Business is no excuse with God. We must take time to stay in the Word on a regular basis. We must evaluate ourselves on this one, Saints! Write it down… estimate just how much time you spend on reading and studying the Bible each day. Compare that to just how much time you spend watching the hell-a-vision…or the television. If you want to be successful, if you want to grow in the Lord, you have to set up a plan and we must stay in the word. We must not allow the enemy to make us think we can do without studying /reading God's word daily! That is one of the devil's playgrounds he sets up in our mind.

We as Christians must step out in faith. I love those words "Step Out" because faith is an action. A lot of Christians think faith is just something you believe. Faith is more than mental assent. It is more than just "knowing"…. it is an action. I can believe a ship will sail and a plane will fly, but it doesn't mean a hill of beans until I get on board. Until I take a step of faith, it means nothing. People can say they believe in God. So what? So does the devil. Faith means that you commit. We commit ourselves to doing something. Action…not just a belief. We can't allow the enemy to play with our minds so that we don't have action behind our faith.

Three times in this passage of scripture we see where God says, "be strong and courageous." Look at verses 6, 7, 9….God told Joshua three times be strong and courageous! Do we as Christians get the message!? There is going to be a lot of things in our lives that will distract us, discourage us, depress us but we MUST be strong and courageous. Step out in faith and don't allow the enemy to place a play-ground of doubt and fear into our mind to the point that we keep wandering around in the wilderness and miss out on the promises that the good Lord has for us. For we see that the children of Israel had been wandering around in the desert for forty years. They had the chance once before , forty years earlier, and they blew it, so God allowed them to wander for forty years. Because they chose to listen to the enemy that placed play-grounds of sin into their lives. We must not allow this to happen in our own lives.

The good Lord does give them another chance. They come to the edge of the Jordan river, and they are ready to cross over into the new land, knowing that the moment they cross that river it's an act of aggression---knowing that the moment they cross over where there are already seven other nations living--- it's an act of war. This means war. The moment they get to the other side all war will break lose. And no telling how long it would last. On the other side there were seven nations, every one of them were larger and much more stronger than the nation of Israel. The nation of Israel didn't have any army. They had been in slavery for 400 years. They were just a bunch of farmers, wives, and children. Now they were about to cross the river and enter into battle and who knows for how long. Now you can see why God was saying, "be strong and courageous." Because He was saying, there are things out there that will tear you down.

Just what gave Joshua the confidence to move ahead? Verse 9...."Remember I have commanded you to be determined and confident! Don't be afraid or discouraged, for I the Lord, am with you wherever you go.""Afraid" and "Discourage."These are two enemies that the devil would love to use as play-grounds in your mind to prevent you from succeeding in life and keeping you from possessing your future with God. These are two things that will keep you from becoming all that God wants you to be----fear and discouragement. See, fear keeps us from getting started. Not ever wanting to try. Thinking that you could never do that sort of thing, etc. Discouragement keeps you from continuing, from finishing what you have begun. We can be hit with a double whammy from the enemy in our minds with fear and discouragement so our lives won't count much....IF we allow him to. We need to stop the enemy from doing this to us in our minds and lives.

Fear and discouragement....they can keep us from being all God wants us to be. God in His Word says... "Don't be afraid, and don't be discouraged! I'm with you." That is the bottom line. It's fear that will keep you in the desert, in the wilderness, when you could be living in the Promised Land of blessings in God. It will keep you from becoming all you can be in God. God says... "Don't be afraid and don't be discouraged!" Let's not allow the enemy to set up a play-ground of fear and discouragement in our minds. For we must resist the devil and his games and he will flee from us. For we have the victory in Jesus!

We as Christians need to have courage!!! Courage is not having any fear in our lives as Christians. Courage is moving on in spite of your fear. We really need to be courageous in God! When you step out in faith in spite of fear and witness to that person on your job or do that assignment you dreaded to do or try that project you always wanted to do or go after that dream or vision you have always had in the back of your mind to try and do someday. You can do it in spite of that fear. We have to put our faith to work in God!

Literally, Joshua and the Israelites had to step out in faith. In chapter 3, when they came up to the Jordan River, it was springtime. The banks of the river were overflowing; it was in the flood stage. God said, "I want you to take the priest. They are to go out in front and carry the Ark of the Covenant. They are to lead the way. I want you to have the priests start walking out into the water, walking across, taking the step of faith, trusting in Me and I will do a miracle." And God didn't give them a hint on how He was going to do it. The Bible says.... "the priests took the Ark of the Covenant in front of the whole nation and began to walk into the Jordan River." Joshua 3:15-16.... "As soon as the priests stepped into the river the water stopped flowing." God had dammed up the river.

This tells us also that the priests had to stand there in the middle of the river while all of the other people passed through, then, and only then, could they {the priests} proceed to go on themselves. These priests had to have extended faith, that the river wouldn't start flowing again until they were safely on the other side. They literally had to "step out" in faith.

This is a lesson for ALL of us to learn. Child of God, the first step is always the hardest one. But don't allow the enemy to set up his mind-games and tell you that you can't do it. It seems always in anything that we try to do the first step seems to be the hardest one for us to take. But don't let that stop you from taken it anyway... "step out" in faith and the Lord will be with you the rest of the way. In writing a book or a term paper, what's the most difficult sentence? The first chapter or the first sentence is the hardest at times. Spiritually, the first step is always the hardest, but we can do all things through Christ Jesus. Don't forget that! Take that initial step and say, "Lord Jesus, I am going to trust You with my life and believe in You and I am not going to allow the devil to set up his play-ground of doubt and fear in my mind. For I have the victory in Jesus!"

What is your Jordan River? What is the barrier in your life that is keeping you from being all that God wants you to be? Where is it in your life? Your career? Is it in a relationship? Something that you are holding onto that you just don't want to let go of? Just what is it that is keeping you in the desert and out of the Promised Land of God's blessings? Just what is it that is so important that it is keeping you from becoming all that God wants you to be? Don't allow the enemy to set up play-grounds in your mind and steal from you what that the Lord has for you in this life and the life here after.

See, Joshua was a man of conviction. Joshua was willing to stand for what was right. He was willing to go against popular opinion. He was willing to do the unusual, the unexpected, and the not so normal thing. Even when the people said to do this, Joshua said... "No, that's not the way the Lord wants me to do it." He was a true man of conviction. The bible spoke about 40 years earlier, of how Moses had chosen 12 spies and they had gone into the Promised Land to spy out the land and they came back. Ten of the spies that Moses sent told him... "we can't do it... there is just no way... they are too powerful and strong for us... they are like giants. They will eat us up. Moses we are like grasshoppers in their sight. We can't do it." But there were two men who said, "We can!" Joshua and Caleb. "We can do it. We can take them out! Let's take them on!" The entire nation said "NO,"... but two men said "YES." It is very interesting, forty years later, God had to let the entire adult population die off and only two of those original people got to go into the Promised Land......Caleb and Joshua.

If we will only listen to what God has told us to do. Preach and teach what He has given us to tell the lost and dying world and not compromise to mankind {and this world's system} God will bless us with a heavenly home.... a Promised Land. Don't allow the devil to set up a play-ground to the point that you listen to man and this worlds way of thinking. Step out in faith go all the way with Jesus and He will go all the way with you. But some of you at this point in your life are saying, "Why should I step out in faith right now? I am pretty comfortable where I am at. I kind of like my life. Why should I shake it up? I am getting too old. My friend, Joshua was 80 years old when God called him to cross the Jordan River and go into battle for the next 25 years.

It's never too late my friend to say "Yes" to God and "No" to the devil. The devil would love to set up his play-ground in your mind so that you would think that you are too old now to do what God has called you to do… what God has placed within your heart to do. But you tell the enemy that it's not too late and that you will do what God has placed within your heart to do. For you have the victory in Jesus to get the job done. Nobody remembers the people who would say, "It can't be done!" We only remember the people who say, "It can!" With God, it can and will be done! Nobody even remembers what the names of the ten spies were…God didn't feel there was even enough room to remember them in greater detail than what He did in the word of God. But everybody remembers the people who step out in faith… like Joshua! Make your life count as Joshua did.

I believe the verse that truly reveals Joshua's character is 24:15…… this is what Joshua said at the end of his life, "Choose for yourselves this day whom you will serve. But as for me and my household we will serve the Lord." Let me ask you this my friend….Have you made that decision in your home? Have you said in some way and some how, this family is going to serve the Lord no matter what comes or goes? This family is going to be a Christian family. It's a choice. Just what kind of person will you be 365 days from now? There maybe some of you who are reading this book that the enemy has plans for you to wash out because he is going to try {or maybe even is already trying at this very moment} to set up his playground in your mind so he can try and destroy your life. But God is saying, "Don't listen to the devil! He is setting you up for a hard fall if you allow him to." God is saying….. "Make your choice but please make it right because I care about you and love you so deeply." The future begins with a commitment my friend. Choose this day whom you are going to serve….God or the devil?

Then in Joshua 3:5 it says… "Then Joshua told the people, Consecrate yourselves, for tomorrow God will do amazing things among you." See they were getting ready to cross the Jordan and Joshua says, "consecrate, dedicate, surrender yourself to God for tomorrow God will do amazing things among us." God is saying to us as Christians get ready for something BIG!. All the past is prologue. The best is yet to come!! Consecrate yourself… for tomorrow God will do amazing things among you. Our lives will have tremendous blessings in these last days before our Lord returns for His bride….the Church. But it will also be a life of battles and fights to get those promised blessings! For even when the children of Israel got into the Promised Land there were still many battles to be fought. Even in the Promised Land there are battles, Saints! But there are blessings, too! And you and I must not allow the enemy to set up a play-ground in our minds to keep us from receiving the blessing that God has for us.

The name Joshua means deliverer, savior. And He was a deliverer for his people. He delivered them into the Promised Land and they beat off all seven nations and thirty-one different kings. His name means deliverer! Thousands of years later, God told Mary to name her boy Joshua. Jesus is the Greek form for Joshua in the Hebrew. Jesus was named after Joshua because He too would be a deliverer! God was saying…. "Just like the great deliverer of old, I am sending a new deliverer to the world."

What's the parallel? The parallel is that the other Joshua (Jesus) wants to take possession of your life. Just like the first Joshua took possession of the promised land, Jesus wants to take possession of your life. Many of you that are reading this book have allowed the Lord to take up possession in your Life. But if you have not allowed Jesus to come into your life, don't put it off another day! Please! See, the devil would love to set up a play-ground in your mind and tell you that you have plenty of time…. "put it off another day" he may be telling you. And if the devil can get that lie through to your mind to put it off just one more day…. soon it will be another day and another and another…. and then, my friend, it will be too late….. the Lord will have already come and you will have been left behind.

My friend, take this first step of faith. Don't allow the enemy to steal it from you another day. I challenge you today to make the devil a liar and make a commitment to Jesus and serve Him with everything you have! Take time to pray…set up some spiritual goals…. read and study the word of God. Tell the enemy that you will not allow him to have your mind {or your life} another day. For you have the victory in Jesus name!

Chapter Eight:
How We Can Make Life Count In Spite Of Our Circumstances

Genesis.39:23 says... "The keeper of the prison looked not to anything that was under his hand; because the Lord was with him, and that which he did, the Lord made it to prosper."

We are going to look at a man named Joseph. A man who really made his life count. He went form a pit to a palace because he listen to God and did not allow the devil to set up play-grounds in his mind to hinder him from becoming all that God wanted him to be. His journey from the pit to the palace was not an easy one at all but he had the victory in Jesus in the midst of it all. He was forsaken by his family, betrayed by his employer and forgotten by his friends. He went from being slave in prison to being the second highest-ranking person in the nation of Egypt, which was the most powerful country at that time. Joseph went from the pit to the palace. His life was a success. This man showed that what counts in life is not your circumstances but your character. There are two things that will determine the quality and success of your life. The choices that you and I make and the character that we display in the face of our circumstances.

Character is that quality that keeps you and I true to our commitment... long after the excitement in which the commitment was made has gone. It is choices and character... not circumstances... that will determine the level of success in our lives. We can make our life count IF we choose to in the Lord. God has big plans for us and we have got to start making our life count.

Just look at the circumstances Joseph had to face. Genesis chapters 37---50 gives us the life of Joseph. His life had it all… revenge, deceit, lust, seduction, attempted murder, violence, attempted rape charges, false charges in prison. Joseph's life would make a great mini series on T.V. He was forsaken and rejected at home. His Dad loved him but no one else really did. He was slandered and seduced at work and his friends had forgotten him.

The first thirty years of his life nothing seemed to be going right. He was rejected at home by his brothers because he was the father's favorite. He was given special things to do that his brothers didn't receive. There was a lot of rivalry, competition and bitterness. Joseph's brothers hated him and were jealous of him. The Bible says that his brothers hated him so much they wouldn't even speak to him in a kind manner at all. And then one day they plotted, "Let's not kill him… let's throw him into this well so he'll die without our having to touch him!" That's really brotherly love, huh?! They did just that! They put him in a well and soon some slave merchants came by whom they sold Joseph to for twenty shekels. He was then taken to Egypt and was sold to a man named Potiphar and became a slave. Over night he went from a pampered son to a slave. My friend, that is really bad rejection by your family. Some of you may have been rejected by your family….look at Joseph….he knew rejection.

And even in the toughest of times Joseph held on to the Lord. He did not give into the devil's whispers and to the play-ground that the enemy was trying so hard to set up in Joseph's mind and life. For Joseph knew in whom he served and if God didn't deliver him out of the hands of his enemies then no one would. For Joseph had the victory in the Lord and he knew it.

Then Joseph started working for Potiphar and he became very successful because he relied on the Lord. Joseph was put in charge of everything in Potiphar's home. But there came a problem soon…. Potiphar's wife got eyes for Joseph. She tried to seduce him and the Bible says, "After a while his master's wife began to desire Joseph and asked him to go to bed with her." But the man of God refused. He did not listen to the enemy. He did not allow the devil to set up any play-grounds of lust into his mind. But each day she would try again and again. She would ask day after day. Sexual harassment in the work place is about 4,000 years old folks! It works both ways… women to men and men to women. But Joseph refused because he listen to God and did not give into the devil's play-ground. He held on to his morals.

Because Joseph did not give into the enemy, in a fit of passion, she grabbed him by the robe, he escaped out of it, losing his coat but keeping his character. That is just what the devil wants us as children of God to do…. lose is our character. But we must not allow him to set up any play-grounds into our minds that will make us do so. See, Potiphar's wife framed Joseph… hell hath no fury like a woman scorned. When Potiphar came home she told him a lie about Joseph she said {my words}, "That Hebrew slave tried to rape me!" That's just like the devil. But Praise God, Joseph still believed in whom he served…God!

So… Joseph was thrown into prison for a crime that he did not commit. He was falsely accused. Set up by lies against him and his character. Here, we see things are going from bad to worse. He gets thrown into prison and there he's forgotten by everyone. But the man of God still holds on to whom and what he believes in. He still did not give into the mind games that the enemy was trying so hard to set up in his mind and life. Joseph was more or less saying, "I would rather die in prison and believe in my Lord than to allow the devil to set me up with his mind games."

While he was in prison, he befriended two of Pharaoh's staff members. And while there Joseph {in my wording} says, "If you get out of this dump, please remember me?" For he had helped them out while there. When one of them was released, he promptly forgot Joseph. "Please be kind enough to mention me to the king and help me get out of this prison?" But the wine steward never gave Joseph another thought--- he forgot all about him. Sometimes jealous and hurtful people will try their best to hurt you, immoral people will try to tempt you and ambitious people will try to use you…. but you can still succeed IF you listen to the Lord and not the devil or you may get discouraged and give up.

But the Lord was with Joseph and gave him success in whatever he did. See… Joseph had a great character. Three times in Genesis 39 it says, "The Lord was with Joseph." Verses 2, 21 and 23 each state that the Lord was with Joseph. Why do you think that the Lord was with Joseph? Was it because he gave into the devil's play-ground of the mind? Or was it because he believed in what God was telling him to do and be? I believe Joseph was quoting this verse in Romans 8:31, "What shall we then say to these things? If God be for me, who can be against me?"

My friend in the Lord, the enemy of your soul and mind will do everything in his power to make your life meaningless and useless. Satan does not want your life to count for anything. Satan does not want your life to influence and impact others. Satan will try and set up a play-ground in your mind to make you think that your life is meaningless and useless in the kingdom of God. We must not allow this to take place in our minds because it is a lie from the enemy. The devil does not want you to win souls for the kingdom of God. My friend, if God is for us, we cannot fail!!! For we have the victory in Jesus Christ!!!

One plus God equals a majority. Why was God with Joseph? Because Joseph was a man of character. What was it about his character that made this man named Joseph so different? What should you and I do when circumstances seem to work against our dreams? What should we do to make our lives count? How can we make an impact when it seems everything is against us to make us fail?

We can do three things…

1. We can fulfill our responsibilities. Wherever we are at that moment in our life, we should do what God has called us to do at that very moment.
2. Maintain our integrity. No matter what happens in our situation, we need to keep our purity and integrity and maintain our moral standards.
3. We must trust in God's sovereignty. You may ask. "What does he mean by trusting God's sovereignty?" It is trusting God's absolute power and control in the affairs of our lives.

If we will do these three things, we will be a successful in spite of our circumstances. We must fulfill our responsibilities, maintain our integrity, and trust in our Lord's sovereignty. And don't allow the enemy to set you up so that we will not fulfill your responsibilities, and maintain your integrity, and trust in your Lord's sovereignty. The enemy would love so very much to set up our minds to the point that we will not do these three important steps.

But Joseph fulfilled His responsibility regardless of his circumstances. Joseph was a very dependable and reliable man of God. He always put his best into everything that he did no matter what the case may have been. And as a result of it all he was promoted to leadership. Never allow the enemy to set your mind up with doubt and fear and tell you that you can't be a leader for God. Joseph did not allow this to take place in his life and as a result he was promoted to leadership.

Genesis 39:6… "And he left all that he had in Joseph's hand; and he knew not ought he had, save the bread which he did eat. And

Joseph was a goodly person, and well favored." We see in this verse that Potiphar gave Joseph complete responsibility over everything he owned. This man did not have a worry in the world with Joseph being there. Joseph made every decision in the house of Potiphar except for what Potiphar would eat. Potiphar had no worries as long as Joseph was there. Can your boss say that about you? See... the Bible says that Potiphar prospered BECAUSE of Joseph. Does your boss proper BECAUSE of YOU?

Then Joseph was thrown into jail. The jailer soon handed over the entire prison administration to Joseph and had no more worries after that, for Joseph took care of everything. You see, if we don't allow the enemy to set up his playground in our minds that we will not come out on the top and be successful in this life, then the Lord will be on our side and bring us out each and every time. Just as he did with this man of God..... he will do for us. So don't allow the devil to tell you any thing different.

Joseph was an incredible guy! You can't keep a godly man down! Joseph gets thrown into prison and the next thing he's assistant warden! For the best of the milk, the cream, rises to the top. If life would have gave him a lemon literally, Joseph would have made lemonade out of it. And in some way Joseph did just that with the Lord's help. Joseph probably said within himself, "I really don't know why these things are happening to me, but one thing I do know and that is how I am supposed to respond." He really didn't know why these circumstances were coming up in his life, but he did know who was Lord of his life. He did not allow the devil to set him up. Whenever anybody turned any responsibility over into Joseph hands, he did have to worry at all... for Joseph was reliable and a man of character.

Do you do your best with the job God has given you to do? Or have you allowed the devil to set up a playground in your mind to make you think that you can't do it? The word of God tells me, I can do all things through Christ Jesus that strengths me. Just keep in your mind that Joseph was in prison on false charges and he starts to rise to the top in that prison. I think Joseph's motto for his life was, make the best of a bad situation. We need to ask to ourselves, "How can I take these circumstances and make them work to my advantage? How can I use these circumstances to make my life better for the Lord?" Let me say, you can either be a victim of your circumstances OR you can be a victor over your circumstances!! The devil would like to set your mind up with his playground so that you will become the victim and not the victor. We must not allow this to take place in our minds.

Joseph kept and maintained his character by fulfilling his responsibility and eventually got his promotion through God. Joseph was victorious over his circumstances. Pharaoh said, "Who can do a better job than Joseph? For he is a man who is obviously filled with the Spirit of God." And this is the reason why in spite of circumstances, Joseph succeeded and ended up second in command in all of Egypt is because wherever he was, no matter where he was serving; Joseph gave it his best shot and didn't allow the enemy to set up any playground in his mind and tell him anything different.

And here is the Law of Success----Luke 16:10, "He that is faithful in that which is least is faithful also in much: and he that is unjust in the least is unjust also in much." See my friends the person who is faithful in the little things will be faithful in big ones and the one who cheats in the little things will cheat in the big things as well.

There are so many people out there that say, "When I make it big THEN I am going to be faithful!" But I say to you who say this: What are you doing with your day to day responsibilities right now? Are you being faithful in the little things? Have you ever heard people say, "When I get out of debt, I am going to start tithing." Just who are they kidding? "When everything settles down in my life, I'll start reading and studying my Bible." Let me say this to the ones that have allowed the enemy to set up this kind of playground in their minds: If you can't be faithful with little responsibility… my God is not going to give you any great responsibility. If we are not faithful in the small things of life, how can God trust us with the bigger things of life?

The Bible tells us in Colossians 3:23, "And whatsoever ye do, do it heartily, as to the Lord ,and not unto men." God always will reward faithfulness in the little things. Some of you might be waiting for that big break! But you haven't been faithful in the little things at this point in your life because the enemy has set up a playground in your mind to cause you to miss out. Today start being faithful in the little things and then God can trust you with much. Tell the enemy from this day forward you will not allow him to keep you back from the blessings of God. That you will be faithful in the little things and for the devil to take his hands off of your mind. Then start giving God the glory and the praise for the victory in your mind for you have been set free. You can succeed in spite of your circumstances!!! First, you fulfill the responsibility… right now… don't wait. Responsibility to God, your family, to church, to your boss, to your nation is a MUST in life IF we are going to make our lives count for God.

Joseph maintained his integrity as well. For Joseph was a man of absolute moral purity. He was a great man of God to the point that they had to lie on him in order to get something to accuse him of. In Genesis 39:10, the boss's wife came to Joseph , "And it came to pass, as she spoke to Joseph day by day, that he hearkened not unto her, to lie by her, or be with her." Joseph did not allow the enemy to set up any temptation in his mind. Joseph maintained his integrity in spite of what the enemy was trying to set up in his life. See…we MUST keep our integrity!!! We must not allow the enemy to set up a playground so that you will lose our integrity. God is well pleased when we hold onto our godly integrity…no matter how hard the hits of the enemy!

Can you imagine the internal battle that must have been going on in Joseph's mind? But he refused to give into the enemy that was trying his best to set up his mind with the playground of lust and temptation…even if he was a slave against his will in a foreign country. Life for Joseph had not gone as he would have liked it to. His dreams had not come true yet. He could have said, "I may as well lose my morals too! Life is just to tough for me to handle! I just owe it to myself to get a lot more pleasure in life. Who cares? What's God done for me? My life is no good… it is going in reverse." Joseph could have said, "I am not upwardly mobile, I am downwardly mobile. Besides, if I befriend the boss's wife, I might even get more promotions." See how the enemy could have been trying to set up playgrounds in Joseph's mind to make him miss out on what God was going to bless him with?

Instead, Joseph did not give in. Joseph might have told the boss's wife, "My master trust me with all that he has in the entire household. How can I do such a wicked thing as what you ask? It would be a great sin against my God!" There were two things that motivated Joseph, the man of God to maintain his integrity.

1.   His loyalty to others and God.
2.   His dear love for God. He could not betray his loyalty to his master.

Joseph was saying that his master had put him in charge of all things. And how could he betray that trust? My friends when you sin you hurt someone else as well as hurting Jesus. Whenever you or I lower our integrity, we hurt other people around us. Joseph was saying, "I will not do what the enemy is trying to set up in my mind to get me to step into and fall! I will not give into the enemy and his playgrounds he is trying to place here to try and destroy my relationship with God as well as the Pharaoh."

In the book of Proverbs 14:32 it says, "The wicked is driven away in his wickedness: but the righteous hath hope in his death." See my friend the wicked people will bring about their own downfall just by doing evil, but good people they are protected by their integrity.

Joseph would not betray his love for God. Joseph's love for God ran much more deeper than his fleshly lust for fame and fortune. The man of God knew that to betray his first love, which was God, was to grieve the very heart of God. Joseph had made up his mind to remain faithful to God regardless of the consequences. Even if he was falsely accused and unjustly imprisoned. Joseph chose not to let the devil set up any kind of a playground in his mind. In spite of it all, this man of God maintained his integrity. We must not allow the enemy to set up his playgrounds in our minds so that we will not keep our integrity. We have the victory in Jesus to keep our integrity. Praise God!

Joseph also trusted in God's sovereignty. Genesis 45:7-8, "And God sent me before you to preserve you a posterity in the earth. So now it was not you that sent me hither, but God." At a very early time in Joseph's life, God gave this young man, Joseph, a dream of making an impact with his life. And this young man shared it with his family. He told his family that God gave him a dream that one day he was going to make him a great king and everyone is going to bow down to him, even his family. But they weren't too excited that their younger brother told them that. It was a right dream but they didn't share good feelings about what Joseph had just said. Sometimes in our lives we might not get the popular vote from people that we are around because of the word that we give them from God. But we must not allow the enemy to set up his playground in our minds so that we will not give out the word that God has called us to give out at that time. See, knowing and hearing the word will set them free... just give it out... for it is the "right now" word.

We can see for thirty years, Joseph's life went downhill. During that thirty years of going downhill, God never explained to him why it was going on in his life. God did not say to him this is what's happening, I am in control and I am planning this and all of these things will work out. So therefore, Joseph was confused. He had no idea what was going on. He had every reason to doubt God's love. He could have said... "But God you gave me that dream. What happened?" He had every reason to be bitter: "Why me God? You gave me a dream and now I have ended up a slave, I am falsely accused of rape, and in prison in a foreign country. Things are not going good for me God." But Joseph kept the vision, the dream that God had given to him. He did not allow the enemy to set up any playgrounds of doubt to the point that he got his eyes off of the dream God showed to him.

Years later it all became clear to Joseph. The word of God tells us that this man of God was eventually promoted to become second in command under Pharaoh. Joseph had interpreted Pharaoh's dream. He told him that… "We are going to have seven years of plenty and then seven years of famine." And Pharaoh's reply was.. "What shall we do Joseph?" And Joseph told Pharaoh… "We should start saving for seven years all the extra crops and put them in storage so that when the seven years of famine comes Egypt will have plenty to eat." Pharaoh said, "Ok, you are in charge! You do it!" So Joseph did according to what God had placed within his mind. He did not allow the enemy to set up playgrounds in his mind to keep them back for having plenty when everyone else was in need and didn't have. See, Joseph was a man of God that listen to the voice of God, for he knew God's voice. The word says that the sheep shall know the master's voice.

Then the Bible says that God blessed Joseph so much that when the seven years of famine came not only did Egypt have more than enough food that they had stored up in advance, but all of the other nations came to Egypt to buy food, and among them were the Israelites. And so many years later, even Joseph's own brothers came to Egypt to buy food from a man not knowing that he was their brother that they had tried to murder and then sold into slavery. What would you and I do in that face-to-face encounter? Would we listen to what the devil would be trying to set up in our minds because we were second in command and we could blow them away? We could order their execution immediately. And so could have Joseph done that to them as well. But he didn't listen to the enemy and his playground of toys he was trying to place in his mind. And we must not listen to what the enemy is trying to set up in our minds either.

There are two very important lessons of life we must learn if we are going to deal with our circumstances effectively….

1. Circumstances often have a hidden purpose. We may not truly understand the circumstances that we face at times in our lives. However, later in our life we can look back and see the hand of God in our circumstances. We will be able to see that God was truly trying to keep us from the pit and get us to the palace.

2. God often will redirect our lives through our circumstances. For God does at times allow circumstances to come into our lives to move us from point A to point B. Because sometimes we have allowed the devil to place a playground of complacency in our minds that we are doing ok where we are at. And then we don't grow spiritually in the Lord anymore. And for doing so God will allow circumstances to arise in our lives to make us a bit uncomfortable so that we will move on with this life of ours' that the Lord is directing... IF we allow Him to do so.

Sometimes as Christians we have allowed the enemy to place a playground in our minds that we have become satisfied with just being saved OR we become satisfied with a certain level of success in our lives. But God's purpose for our life is to impact and change the world where we live. So if we are going to impact and change the world we need to start where we live.

Joseph said, "My God sent me ahead of you." Notice his reaction to his brothers who had tried to kill him. Genesis 50:20, "But as for you, ye thought evil against me; but God meant it unto good, to bring to pass, as it is this day, to save much people alive." Let me say this... many of you who are reading this book have been harmed by other people----a former spouse, a parent, a brother or sister, a teacher, boss, a former girlfriend---they meant to harm you. There is no doubt about it! They meant to harm you! But my God can turn it around for your good if you will only let Him. For God has a plan that is much more greater than your problem. Don't allow the devil to set up his playground in your mind and make you think anything different. For God has a plan for you and you have the victory in Jesus.

There is a word that seems to be the most popular word around today and it is the word "victim." But let me just say this... in Christ you don't have to stay a victim. You can be a victor! See, those people mean it for bad but God means it for the good in our life. That is a fact of life. You and I don't have to allow what people have done to us in our past to continue to hurt us. People and the devil meant it for the bad but God is greater then those people and God meant it for good. Don't allow the devil to set up a playground of hurt from the past experiences and guilt of past sins in your mind to the point that you think you are no good to God. You have the victory in Jesus and you have been forgiven. Don't allow the devil to tell you anything different.

73

And I think a lot of the problem with some Christians is they have allowed the devil to place a playground of bitterness, the root of bitterness, into their minds. For bitterness is refusing to trust in God's sovereignty. It will say, "I don't really think God has my best interest at heart....I don't really think God's in control....I am so bitter because this is happening to me and I don't think God knows what He's doing by allowing it." Let me make one thing clear... I didn't say that God causes it all. He didn't. You might be asking, "What about all the sin in the world?" Well, God gives us all the freedom to choose to do good or to do bad. For He chooses to allow us to have freedom of choice. As a result, some innocent people do get hurt in the crossfire. That's the bad news. But the good news is that my God can turn it all around for our good! People may mean it to harm you in some way, but God will turn it all around for good to develop in your life if we trust in Him and let Him come in to do just that! And He will make you into what He wants you to be.......that very special jewel of His with the character He wants you to have. You will become a better individual in God due to that hurt, etc. My wife, Renee, and I have learned this to be truth!

My friends, Joseph had a persistent faith. He was waiting for years for his dream to come true. For thirty years nothing was going right for this man of God. Even when Joseph didn't understand, he trusted God and the dream that God had showed him as a young man. Where did his dream get him? His dreams got him into slavery. Where did his integrity get him? His integrity got him into prison. Where did his helping others get him? Nowhere....at first But you didn't see this man of God become bitter, having a pity party. Because he did not allow the devil to set up his playgrounds into his mind. We see the man of God doing his responsibility, doing his very best he could do with what he had, and doing his best wherever he was. You see him maintaining his integrity. He may lose his dream at first, but he was not going to lose his morals. You see this man of God trusting in God's sovereignty. He knew God had a plan. And he was not going to allow the devil to place a playground in his mind and tell him anything different.

I know God has a plan for you and I, but we must not allow the enemy to place a playground within our minds and tell us anything different about it. Because they would be all lies! Let me say this... just what do you do when circumstances dispute the dreams that God has given you? You should do what Proverbs 3:5-6 says, "Trust in the Lord with all thine heart; and lean not unto thine own understanding. In all thy ways acknowledge him, and he shall direct thy path." We need not to try and figure it out ourselves. We just need to trust in God, because he will help us. Just ask Him.

When we are going through a circumstance that we don't like, we need to ask ourselves these three questions…

1. Is it my fault? A lot of times we bring it on ourselves.
2. What can I learn from this circumstance?
3. How does my God want me to act in this circumstance?

I believe Philippians 1:27 summarizes Joseph's life. Whatever happens, make sure that your everyday life is worthy of the gospel of Christ.

It's not so much what happens to us, but what happens in us. It's not so much your circumstances, but your character that makes you great. And whatever happens, make sure your everyday life is worthy of the gospel. For one of the top secrets of Joseph's success is that he honored God everyday----in the trivial, the day to day chores he honored his God in all he did. What kind of circumstances have you allowed the devil to place as a playground in your mind that you use as an excuse for not doing more in your life for God. What has the devil made you use as an excuse? You may be asking, "How can I maintain my integrity? I have already lost it." Start over my friend. God is a God of "starting over". Let the blood of Christ make you and your mind clean and pure before Him. Don't be ashamed to go to Him for He loves you so much and is more than willing to help you.

Some of you may be saying, "I can't make an impact with my life. I have failed with my life." So what? Study the Bible and you will find out the people God used the most had major flaws and failures in their lives. But yet God used them because God loves to show Himself mightily to humanity. Don't allow the enemy to use past failures in your mind as an excuse. Because you have been forgiven and you have the victory over the playgrounds that the devil has tried to set up in your mind. Just give God the praise for it all.

Chapter Nine:
How You Can Benefit Your Mind Through The Bible

Our lives are to be governed and controlled by the word of God… the Bible. Yet there are many in our churches through out America and the rest of the world who have allowed the devil to place his playgrounds of fear, doubt, unbelief, wrong emotions and bad feelings in their minds in order to keep them from reading God's divine word. And we must not allow the devil to overtake us with such things. For the devil also knows it doesn't matter how much or how many Bible verses you can quote from memory. Don't get me wrong here, we do need to know and commit God's word to memory and to our lives, but unless we actually USE IT and APPLY IT to our daily lives it will not benefit us at all. We will only experience the blessings and the benefits of the Bible as we apply it to our lives and our circumstances.

There are so many people that mark their Bibles but they do not allow the Bible to mark them. As we study God's word….. God's word will study us. The book of James 1:25 says, "But whoso looketh into the perfect law of liberty, and continue therein, he being not a forgetful hearer but a doer of the work, this man shall be blessed in his deed." The Bible is called the perfect law because it is exactly what we need. It promises freedom and blessings to those that will receive it. Receive God's word today and every day of your life.

James gives us three steps on how to benefit from the Bible…

1.   There must be a willingness for us to receive the word of God.

James 1:21 says, "Wherefore lay apart all filthiness and superfluity of naughtiness and receive (accept) with meekness the engrafted word which is able to save your souls." "Receive" in the Greek is a hospitality term which literally means "to openly welcome the word"…"come on in". If we are going to ever benefit from the word of God, then we must welcome the word of God into our lives. And not allow the devil to set up his playground of thoughts that we don't have to welcome the word of God into our life or have the willingness to receive it into our lives. In order for us to benefit from God's word, it must gain access into our lives. James tells us it is the engrafted word. In other words, it is planted in us when we receive it.

In Matt. 13, Jesus told the parable of the sower and the seed. Jesus said that the word of God is the seed and the soil is our heart. And in this parable, Jesus gives us three conditions of the heart that will hinder the effectiveness of God's word in our lives. And then He gives you and I the right heart condition.

1.   The heart is unprepared to receive the seed. Meaning that they hear the word but don't understand it. The devil sets up his playground in their minds and he comes and steals it away. We must not allow this to take place.
2.   The hardened heart. they hear the word and receive the word with joy. But it doesn't last long for when the enemy brings trouble they are offended because of the word which cuts out the bad fruit in our lives to help us grow in the Lord. This reveals lack of commitment to stand when faced with trouble.
3.   The crowded heart. The cares of this old world and the deceitfulness of riches choke the effectiveness of God's word in our lives. The word of God is crowded out. This person is too busy trying to gain the wealth and prosperity of the world and has no time for God's word.
4.   The prepared heart. The ground has been cultivated and watered with prayer. The weeds have been pulled to make room for the word of God.

How is it you can take two seeds that are of the same fruit, exactly the same, and plant them in two different locations and get two different crops in fruit? Well, one soil is prepared and the other one is not. Then how is it that you can take two people and put them in the same service and hear the same message and one person gets blessed by the message and receives it and the other person says they didn't get anything out of it? Well, one heart was prepared and the other heart was not. We can not allow the devil to set up our minds so that we will not receive from God the blessings that He has for us.

James was saying that we must receive the word of God with the right heart attitude. And he tells us how to prepare our hearts to receive the word of God.

A. We must listen very carefully. Hebrews 2:1, "So we must listen very carefully to the truths we have heard, or we may drift away from them (The Living Bible.)." We must listen carefully to the word of God....James1:19, "Be swift {quick to listen} to hear." We must give it our full attention. Don't allow the enemy to take your mind off of what God wants you to hear for your life from the word of God. This is one of the devil's playgrounds that he would love to place within your mind so that you will not listen to the voice of God. The word of God is God's voice talking to us. We must be alert! We must not miss it on what God wants to tell us. Slow to speak. Many of our problems are caused because we're quick to speak rather than being quick to listen. We must learn to listen carefully to God's word. Be ready. Be intent on hearing it. Be ready to receive God's word. Be careful. We must not allow the enemy to place playgrounds in our minds so that we will not listen carefully to the word of God.

Do you know of someone that you share the word of God with and rather them carefully listening, they are acting like and thinking how they are going to reply back to what God's word says. "Brother/ Sister _____, I know that the word of God says that. But what about this or what about that." These people they are always looking for loop holes in God's word. This is because they have allowed the devil to set up a playground in their mind that gives them an excuse to try and release them from their responsibility in obeying God's word. There is no loop holes in God's word. So we must not allow the enemy to set up anything different in our minds to the contrary.

B. We must remain calm. James 1:19 says, " to be slow to wrath." If we are going to receive God's word and be blessed by it we must be slow to wrath...not get angry because of the word which convicts or corrects us. A calm and peaceful attitude will allow us to be more receptive to God's word. If we are relaxed, people can communicate with us more. The anger spoken of here is anger towards God's word and the messenger of God {one who is speaking God's word}. When some people need correction in their lives they don't appreciate or welcome the word of God that brings correction. See, the devil has set up his playground in their minds so that they will not receive the correction that they need to grow more spiritually with God. Don't ever allow this to take place in your mind and life.

The word for "anger" here means "a seething anger that only you {and God} know about. It is not a "blow up" anger. This is an anger that causes you to be secretly upset, bitter and resentful. And all this is a set up of the devil's playground in your mind to get you off of what is important in God and to your life in God. James was saying {in my own words}, "Don't get upset with God's word and his messenger. Don't be bitter at God's word or his messenger. Don't resent God's word or his messenger. Allow the word of God to do it's work in you and be blessed by it.

We tend not to hear much when we are anger, resentful, bitter, and upset. Bitterness can be a barrier, an emotional block that will keep us from hearing God's words. You may ask, "How come God never speaks to me?" It could be that you have some resentment in your life that you need to get rid of. James says to be calm, be slow to anger. We must not allow the enemy to set up his playground of resentment, anger, and bitterness in our minds because once we receive it into our minds then it will go to our heart and then it will come out of us in some shape or form. It won't be pretty when it happens either!

What is your emotional state when you go to church? Do you have a calm attitude? Or do you come angry with someone? And if you come to church with anger in your heart towards a family member, have had a argument with your spouse/children, or come angry with someone at the church, you will not receive any blessings until you get it right with God and those you are angry with. And allow the word of God to sink in and change you. See, your anger will not accomplish God's right purpose. For James 1:20 says, "The wrath (anger) of man worketh not the righteousness of God." So we must not allow the enemy to place his playground of anger and bitterness into our lives to the point that we miss out on the blessings of God.

C. We must be clean. James 1:21 says, "Wherefore lay apart all filthiness and superfluity of naughtiness" ....Before you can plant the seed you have to do a little weeding. The word "filth" that he is using means in the Greek "ear wax." In other words, get the wax out…clean your ears of all that the enemy has placed as a playground in you. When the enemy places a playground in your mind, it blocks your spiritual hearing and keeps you back from receiving what God has for you at that time. It prevents God's word from getting down into your heart. He says to get rid of the evil "stinking thinking" that the enemy has placed there. For our God tells us to lay aside all emotional garbage, the old habits, the junk in your life that the enemy has used in you as his playground so that God's word can get through to you.

You must get rid of those things that would hinder you from hearing God's word. How can we be clean? By our confession. If we confess our sins he is faithful and just to forgive us and cleanse us of all unrighteousness. Don't allow the devil to keep you back from confessing your sins. He will place a playground in your mind that will say that, "It's ok… you haven't did no big sin." My friend, sin is sin! There is no "big sin" and no "little sin" in God's eyes… sin is sin to Him.

D. We must be willing to comply. We have to be teachable, humble, yielded, willing to be changed. Humbly accepting the word of God planted in you. And don't act like you know it all, for if you think you know it all, God's word can't get through to you. We need to pray, "God, you do what you need to do in my life to make me the Christian you want me to be." God is saying if you and I want to be blessed and benefit from his word, first we have to receive it. Receiving God's word it just isn't enough.

2. We must have a willingness to reflect on the word of God.

James 1:23, "For if any be a hearer of the word, and not a doer, he is like unto a man beholding his natural face in a glass." James is using an illustration here. He says God's word is like a mirror. And the purpose of the mirror is for us to evaluate ourselves. We look into a mirror to access the damage from the night before. Then we do something about it. For what good is a mirror if you don't do anything about it after you look into it? God says a mirror reflects what and whom we are on the outside. God's word reflects what we are like on the inside. And a lot of times some Christians don't even know what they are on the outside let alone who they are on the inside because they have allowed the enemy to set up a playground. They can't see through the mirror. They have allowed the enemy to shatter the mirror to pieces.

Have you ever seen yourself in the mirror of the Bible? I know I have and so has my wife, Renee. Hebrews says, God's word can detect the thoughts, intents, and desires of the heart. A lot of Christians don't read the bible because they're afraid. They're unwilling to face themselves in the mirror of God's word and see themselves as they really are…the way God sees them on the inside. They really don't want to look at the mirror of God's word. The devil has set his playground up in their minds. Don't allow this to take place in your life my friend.

There are three was for us to reflect on God's word that James gives us to follow.

A. We must read and study God's word. James 1:25, "But whoso (man, woman, boy, or girl) looketh into the perfect law." Here James is talking more about research than he is reading. Investigating. The word "look" in Greek means "to stoop down and gaze in." We must focus our attention on the word of God. We must not allow the enemy to place a playground up so that we will get our attention off of the word of God and what God has to tell us. There are two ways you and I can look at a mirror: we can gaze at it OR we can glance at it. When we just glance at it we quickly walk away and forget what we have seen. It didn't do us any good. Many have tried to have a quite time in God's word that way. They don't want to gaze at it, but glance at it. They won't even give God two minutes. God says he wants us to gaze at the word. To look at it intently in detail.

That's how we must look at God's word... in detail. Look at the details. James was saying we need so very much to receive God's word and reflect upon it. First by reading and studying it then by reviewing it. We must review the word of God. James 1:25, "and continue therein." This means over and over again. This is called meditation. When we think of something over and over again this is called meditation. "Meditation" means "to think seriously about something over and over again." Let me say this, if you know how to worry... you can meditate. If we take a negative idea and we began to think on it over and over again... it's called worry. But take God's word and think it over and over again and it's called meditation. The Bible says to meditate on God's word. Jesus said if you continue in my word, then you are truly my disciples. Saints of God, read it and reread it and review it. If you want to be blessed by the word receive it and don't allow the devil to set up his playground of doubt and disbelief in your mind to stop you from meditating on God's truth in His word.

Psalm 119:97 says, "O how I love thy law! It is my meditation all the day." Do you want to prosper and have good success? Then meditate upon the word of God. Joshua 1:8 says, "This book of the law shall not depart out of my mouth; but thou shall meditate therein day and night, that thou may observe to do according to all that is written therein: for then thou shall make thy way prosperous, and then thou shall have good success." The devil doesn't want you to be prosperous and have great success. So he starts to set up a playground in your mind so that you will not study /meditate upon the word of God. The devil will try to keep you back from the blessings that God's word has for you. Don't allow this to happen! Resist the devil and his playgrounds of the mind and he will have to flee from you. Because you have the victory in Jesus' name. This is a promise... if we meditate on God's word, we will be prosperous and we will have good success.

People of God, read God's word...review it continually. Stay in it and be faithful to the word of God. I know some that are more faithful to Readers Digest than they are to God's word. We need to fill our minds with the word of God. James is saying, "Do you want to benefit from God's word?" Reflect on God's word. Think on it by reading, studying it and reviewing it. And don't allow the enemy to place any kind of playgrounds in your mind to get you sidetracked from it.

As Christians we MUST remember God's word. James 1:25, "Not being a forgetful hearer." We will benefit spiritually and physically from God's word, IF we start memorizing scripture so we can apply it to our daily lives and the daily circumstances we find ourselves in. It will benefit us on a personal level and on a spiritual level in developing the habit of memorizing Scripture for the purpose of growth and development. "Thy word {God} have I hid in my heart that I might not sin against thee." We need to memorize God's word if we want to benefit from it. Take notes. Write things down if necessary! If you value God's word you will write things down. Then study what you have written down. Don't allow the devil to take you for a ride in your mind. It is very important to know the things that God's word says about what He wants us to do.

3. We must have a willingness to respond to the word of God.

James 1:22-24, "But be ye doers of the word, and not hearers only, deceiving your own selves. For if any be a hearer of the word, and not a doer, he is like unto a man beholding his natural face in a glass: For he behold himself, and goes his way, and straightway forgets what manner of man he was." Understand here what James is saying, if you and I are not doing what the word says we are deceiving ourselves.

What good is a mirror if we don't look at it and don't do anything about how we look afterwards? When we gaze into the mirror we see the real person. We see where we need to make improvements. James says we see our natural face. In other words, we see the face that we were born with. When we study God's word, we will see all our imperfections, our weaknesses, our short comings and our sin. But the wonderful news is, when we study God's word, it also reveals what we need to do to correct all these problems. God's word shows us our sin and then shows us the solution to it. We are deceiving ourselves when we hear the word and we don't apply the word to correct the problem.

Don't allow the devil to place any kind of a playground in your mind that you will not correct the problems in your life when you hear the word of God spoken unto you/or when you read/study it yourself. For this is just what the devil would like for you to do. So that you will not be blessed of God and do His will for your life.

My honest prayer for you, the reader of this book, is that you will remember what God the Father has given you in this chapter {and book} and that you will put it to practice in your daily walk in God. That you would be a Living, Walking Bible. And the best translation of the Scripture is when you translate it into your life and let it change you. Don't allow the devil to set you up another day with any of his playground toys in your mind. Take back what the enemy has been trying to steal from you. For you have the victory in Jesus Christ.

Chapter Ten:
We Need To Watch Our Words

We all should know the old saying, "Sticks and stones may break my bones, but words will never hurt me." I am here to tell you that is not a true statement. Words, my friend, do hurt. Broken bones can heal over a period of time. But it takes so long for us to get over hurtful words said to us. Some people never recover from the crushing words spoken to them from others. I can tell you of people today who are living in defeat and depression because of words that were spoken to them as they were growing up. I can tell you of people that believe that they are worthless, no good, and will never amount to anything because that is just what they were told growing up as a child. And that makes them still suffer from the verbal abuse that they received as a child. Don't allow the devil to set up this playground of hurt in your mind that you will end up speaking them out and hurting the people around you, too, even the ones you love dearly. My friends in the Lord, the words we speak effect the world around us. What we say and how we communicate with each other has lasting results...good or bad!

Did you know the words we speak can give life, hope, and love. Or the words we speak can bring death, division, and destruction. Proverbs 18:21 says, "Death and life are in the power of the tongue." Once those words are gone out of our mouth it is too late. Do you believe with me that this is why James said that we are to be quick to hear, slow to speak and slow to anger? In other words, engage your brain before you engage your mouth!!! Study the words that you are about to say. Are they playgrounds that the enemy is getting ready to use out of you to hurt someone? And if so, don't give into that playground. And by all means, don't let what you say be the result of anger. Because when we get angry, we say things we know that we shouldn't say and later regret what we say.

WARNING! WARNING! There is a tongue loose out there! WARNING! Please…watch your words carefully. Think before you speak! The tongue is in a wet place and it can slip easily! Matthew 12:36-37 says, "But I say unto you, That every idle word that men shall speak, they shall give account thereof in the day of judgment. For by thy words thou shall be justified, and by thy words, thou shall be condemned." The taming of the our tongue and a careful watch over our speech is very important that the word of God gives us instructions concerning. Let us take the warnings in the word of God about our speech seriously and not allow the enemy to set us up for any of his mind games of hurt.

James told us that a mature Christian is:

*Patient in trouble times.

*Practices the truth.

*And now he is telling us that a mature Christian has power over the tongue.

James 3:2 says, " If any man offend not in word, the same is a perfect (mature) man." We can measure the maturity of a Christian by the content of their speech. Paul said in 1 Corinthians 13:11, "When I was a child , I spoke as a child, I understood as a child, I thought as a child: but when I became a man, I put away childish things."

Let's just look and see what God says to us about our tongues and our words and why must we watch what we say. Why must you and I do that? Have you ever heard these before? "It's just words"… "I'm just kidding"… "All I am doing is just playing with you." And that is just it! You are playing with them… just like the devil has been playing with your mind and you are getting ready to hurt that person. James was saying words are significant. Three reasons we have to learn to manage our mouth. Then James gives us six illustrations: two for each of the points. James was such a great communicator because he knew how to illustrate what God was giving him to say.

A. Our words can direct us and others in life.

Because it has a tremendous influence and control over our lives. Just where are you headed in this life? And where will you be ten years from now? Just look at your conversation. Just what is it that you like to talk about? What is it that you talk about the most in your life? Did you know that you can shape your words… then your words shape you. Please don't allow the enemy to place his playground of words in your mind to where you shape your words around him and those words then shape you.

James says the tongue is small, it's tiny. And a lot of people think just because it's tiny, it's insignificant. But it does have tremendous power… James 3:3. Consider a bit in a horse's mouth. Say you have a stallion, 1,000-2,000 pounds, and a 90 pound jockey on his back. This jockey can control that tremendous mighty horse by just a little piece of metal stuck strategically over his tongue. My point is… your tongue controls the direction of your life wherever you want to go, and just a little bit of a word or a phrase can influence the total direction of your life. But don't allow the enemy to set you up this way and place his bit in your mouth… a bit of a word or a phrase so that he will direct your life.

A ship weighing thousands of pounds is directed by one small rudder. Even in the midst of the storms the rudder still guides the ship. Did you know that your words have the same power to direct people to Jesus or away from Jesus. There are so many people in this world that think, if the tongue has such influence maybe it's best to say nothing. Not to talk at all, just be silent. But see that also can be a playground that the enemy has placed within your mind to keep you from telling people about the Lord and helping people with just some kind words.

B. Our words can destroy us and others.

James 3:5 says, "Even so the tongue is a little member, and boast great things. Behold, how great a matter a little fire kindles." For a moment, imagine with me a beautiful forest…..trees everywhere. But imagine it all of a sudden up in smoke, completely destroyed instantly with one tiny little match. It only takes a spark to get a fire going. James was saying that your tongue can also destroy like that. You can lose it all. One little match in the wrong hands can destroy an entire forest overnight. And a careless word can destroy a life overnight. Think about it!

Lives can be destroyed. Gossip is like a fire. It can spread quickly and it wrecks havoc. Just how many people have, because of careless words, destroyed their marriage, career, reputation, or the reputation of another, or church, or friendship. It turns my stomach to even think of it. The tongue not only has the power to direct you where to go but it can also destroy what you have if you don't learn to control it. It's like a fire remember?! Don't allow the devil to set your mind up with this playground so that it will destroy what you have with your family and most of all what you have with God. For the devil would love to get you in this area. But you don't have to allow it another day for you can have the victory in Jesus. Let the enemy know that.

Also our words can be devastating to others. Proverbs 18:21, "Death and life are in the power of the tongue." Job !9:2, "How long will you vex my soul, and break me in pieces with words." James 3:6, "And setting on fire the course of nature; and it is set on fire of hell." James is saying here that words can create a chain reaction....a domino effect. We can say something that we didn't mean to have any harmful effects whatsoever but it can have devastating effects that is beyond our control.

Our words can become a chain reaction of hurtful events... the course of hell. If we don't become aware of the playgrounds that the enemy is trying to set up in our minds to hurt other people, that is just what we will do. It will be the course that the devil has placed within your mind... one of his playgrounds to hurt and destroy you and the people around you. Don't allow this to take place in your life. Because our words can be set on fire by hell itself. James was saying we have to learn to manage our mouths. Not only can it direct where we are to go but it can destroy what we already have. We can lose our family, our kids, our career, etc., simply by what we say. It's like a fire from hell itself God's word tells us. Let's not allow the devil to set us up so that he will destroy everything that we have.

Proverbs 21:23 says, "Whoso keeps his mouth and his tongue keeps his soul from trouble."

Ephesians 4:29-30 says, "Let no corrupt communication proceed out of your mouth, but that which is good to use of edifying {lifting up}, that it may minister grace unto the hearers. And grieve not the Holy Spirit of God, whereby ye are sealed unto the day of redemption." Paul is saying {here in Ephesians} when we use words that hurt and tear people down rather than building them up we are grieving the precious Holy Spirit of God. And let me tell you, God is not pleased with our words because we are not building up our brothers/sisters in the Lord or those we may come across in this world we see every day. We must build up our brothers/sisters in the body of Christ and not allow the enemy to place his playgrounds of hurt into our minds to try and destroy or hurt them in any kind of way. For if we do allow this to take place we are grieving the Holy Spirit of God. Let's not allow this to happen friends.

We need to pray the prayer of the Psalmist. Psalm 19:14 says, "Let the words of my mouth, and the meditation of my heart, be acceptable in thy sight, O Lord, my strength, and my redeemer." This should be our hearts prayer. So that we don't allow the enemy to have his way with our minds and words.

James goes on to say this in James 3:7 & 8, "For every kind of beast, and birds, and of serpents, and of things in the sea, is tamed, and hath been tamed of mankind: But the tongue can no man tame; it is an unruly evil, full of deadly poison." It is like poison. The word "poison" in the Greek is "snake venom." Only a few drops will kill. Did you know you can assassinate someone with your words. Assassinate their character. For the tongue is a deadly weapon. We have to be very watchful not to allow this type of playground to enter our minds then come out of our lips. For this is just what the devil would love to do to us is use our mind and then our mouth to assassinate someone's character and crush them devastatingly.

The word of God says no man can tame the tongue. No man! But I know one who did and still can! Jesus Christ!!! For He is able to tame and control a lying, blaspheming, slanderous, gossiping, backbiting and destructive tongue. Just as much as He is able to deliver the drug addict from drugs, the gambler from his gambling, the drunkard from his alcohol. God is an awesome God and He can do anything that we allow Him to do in us. But there has to be a willingness on our part to yield and surrender our tongues over to the Lord and the Holy Spirit. We can overcome! We don't have to allow the enemy to set up this playground. For the word of God tells us in James 4:7, "Submit yourselves therefore to God. Resist the devil, and he will flee from you." See, my friend, we can and do have the victory in Jesus! Just submit!!

Also our words can display who we are and what's in our hearts. It can reveal our real character. And it tells what's really inside of us. James points out how inconsistent we are in our speech. James 3:9-10 says, "Therewith bless we God, even the Father; and therewith curse we men, which are made after the similitude {likeness} of God. Out of the same mouth proceeded blessing and cursing. My brethren, these things ought not so to be." My friends, we say these things out of the same mouth....blessings and cursing. We go to church and we praise God. We will sing praises to the Lord in songs. And then we walk out, get into our cars and on the way home we argue about where we are going to eat lunch. Isn't it just amazing how quickly our attitudes can change? In one minute, we are so happy, singing and praising God and the next minute, we are saying, "Will you just shut up already!" It's so inconsistent. Just see how the enemy can set you up with his playground within your mind to make you a Dr Jekyll and Mr.Hyde? Don't allow it!! Stop the devil in his tracks!

One minute we are praising God and the next minute we are cursing other people. Cursing doesn't just necessarily mean profanity. But it does mean any kind of put down or bad labeling. "You're just like _____"…."You good for nothing"…."You'll never amount to nothing". Any kind of put down is a curse. James is says, "Why curse men? They are made in God's image." Saints, these are labels (playgrounds) that the enemy will set up to get you to use on people to the point it will hurt them and in some cases destroy them. We must not allow this to happen.

Then James gives us an answer in verse 11-12, "Doth a fountain send forth at the same place sweet water and bitter? Can the fig tree, my brethren, bear olive berries? Either a vine, figs? So can no fountain both yield salt water and fresh." The point that he was saying was this… whatever is in the well comes out in the water. And whatever is in the tree, comes out in the fruit. What is the likelihood of a cherry tree producing apples? Zero! Zip!

What's inside our heart is what comes out. And then the mouth eventually betrays what is really on the inside. See, the devil will set us up with this playground in our mind and then from there {if we allow it} will go to the heart and from the heart the mouth speaks and it is going to let others know what's really inside.

Have you ever heard this excuse? Someone has just said something really mean and hurtful and they say, "I really don't know what came over me or what got into me?""It's not like me to say that.""I don't know why I said that.""I really didn't mean it." But James would say, "Yes, it is. It's just like you on the inside. You did mean it. Stop kidding yourself. For what's inside your heart is going to come out." We can't have a spring that one minute it gives out salt water and the next minute it gives out fresh water. That's inconsistent. It's comes naturally to you. What is in a well comes out of the well. So what is in us… will come out of us. We must not allow the devil to set up this type of playground in us.

Jesus himself said in Matthew 12:34, "For out of the abundance of the heart the mouth speaks." He is saying here that what's inside of you is what's going to come out. Our tongue just displays what we are. And it directs where we go. It can destroy what we have. But most of all, it displays who we are and what's really in our hearts. It reveals our true character. So if we want to be known as having a great character, a godly character, we must not allow the devil to set up this playground within us and then allow it to go to our hearts, and from there, speak them out to just end up hurting others and ruining our lives.

Our words can delight others so that they can be blessed and not hurt/destroyed. Proverbs 18:4 says, "The words of a man's mouth are as deep waters, and the wellspring of wisdom as a flowing brook." Proverbs 12:18 says, "But the tongue of the wise is health." Proverbs 12:25 says, "Heaviness in the heart of man makes it stoop: but a good word makes it glad." Proverbs 25:11 says, "A word fitly spoken is like apples of gold in pictures of silver." Our words can refresh and encourage someone that is discouraged and about ready to give up and quit. Our words can give new life to a dying relationship. So we must not allow the devil to place any kind of playground like this into our minds. We can be a huge help to hurting people just by a simple, kind word.

What the solution is:

Is for people to get a new heart. People have got to get a new heart! That's the problem…too many Christians walking around with an old heart still…no change in it. Ezekiel 18:31, "Cast away from you all your transgressions, whereby ye have transgressed; and make you a new heart and a new spirit." Painting the outside of the well doesn't make any difference if there is poison in the well. We can change the outside of us, we can turn over a new leaf, but what we really need is a new heart and life. What we need is a fresh start. We need to let go of all the past and be born again and start over. We need to get a new heart. And don't allow the enemy to place a playground within your mind to keep you back from receiving that new heart.

You may ask, "How do I get a new heart?" 2 Corinthians 5:17 says, "Therefore if any man be in Christ, he is a new creature: old things are passed away; behold, all things are new." And my friends, ALL means ALL!!! A new heart, a new life, new spirit. When you come to Jesus Christ , He wipes out everything you have ever done in the past. He says it's time to start anew. It's like you are being born again but this time it is spiritually being born again. You need a new heart. See, this is why the devil loves to set up his playgrounds in your mind because he knows if he can get your mind… he can get the heart as well. Don't allow this to happen to you. Start praying like David did in Psalm 51… Create in me a clean heart, O God, because what's in my heart will come out of my mouth.

Ask God for help every day. There is no shame in it. We NEED supernatural power! So we ask God to help us. Psalm 141:3 says, "Set up a watch, O Lord, before my mouth; keep the door of my lips." You can't do it on your own. Our messed up life at one time is living proof of that. And if your life is messed up due to what I have written in this chapter, than you need to do what God and I are telling you through this chapter. For we cannot control it on our own. You should quote this every morning: "God, put a muzzle on my lips. Guard my lips and mouth. Don't let me be judgmental today. Don't let me be critical today. Don't let me say things that I will most definitely will regret." We need to ask God for help daily because we need his power in our life daily. Stop allowing the devil to set you up with his playground toys and keep you back from the blessings of God.

Getting into God's word is a big way of asking God for help. As you step out and ask God for his help, start reading the word and the enemy will have to flee your mind. He will have to take up his playground and all his toys that he has been using on you for such a long time and he will have to go. Fill your mind with the word of God…positive things, whatsoever things are true, etc., think on these.

We need to think before we speak . We need to engage our minds before engaging our mouth. James 1:19 says, "Be swift to hear, slow to speak, slow to wrath (anger)." What does your tongue say about you? What does it reveal about your character? If you played back a tape of every conversation that you have had this past week, what would you learn about yourself? God hears it all. What direction is your tongue leading you? Maybe you need to ask forgiveness. Maybe you need to go to your kids to say I am sorry. Maybe you need to apologize to your wife or your husband. Let me say this… whatever it is that you need to do… just do it. Don't allow another day to go by with the enemy placing this playground within your mind so that you will not be set free from the bondage that he has you in at this time. For you can have the victory over these areas the enemy has you bound in. You can have the victory through Jesus Christ! Give Jesus the praise and glory for it!

Chapter Eleven:
The Signs Of Maturity In Your Mind

Maturing and growing in God is not an option. In fact, it is God's will for every believer to grow and mature in order to become more like the Lord Jesus Christ. In Hebrews 6:1 it says, "Let us go on unto perfection (maturity)." God is telling us to grow up! 2 Peter 3:18 says, "But grow in grace, and in the knowledge of our Lord and Savior Jesus Christ." We MUST grow up! It is NOT an option… it is a command. And the purpose for the church is to help Christians grow and become more like the Lord Jesus Christ. We must not allow the enemy to set up this playground in our minds to where we get our mind off of what God has called us to do. We, as a body of believers, are to help the weaker brothers/sisters in the faith. We aren't doing this if we are tearing each other down.

Look at what the Apostle Paul says in Ephesians 4:11-14, "And he gave some, apostles; and some, prophets; and some, evangelists; and some, pastors and teachers. For the perfecting of the saints, for the work of the ministry, for the edifying of the body of Christ. Till we come in the unity of the faith, and of the knowledge of the Son of God, unto a perfect man, unto the measure of the fullness of Christ. That we henceforth be no more children, tossed to and fro, and carried about with every wind of doctrine, by the sleight of men, and cunning craftiness, whereby they lie in wait to deceive." Saints, there is a whole message in this passage of scripture. It is sufficient to say that the reason God gave these gifted people to the church is to bring the church to maturity. If God has called you as a prophet, evangelist, pastor, teacher, don't allow the enemy to place a playground within your mind to keep you back from what God has called you to do.

Before we go into what maturity is… lets look at what maturity isn't.

What maturity is not:

Maturity has nothing to do with your age… if you are old or young. Saints, it has nothing to do with how long a person has lived or how long a person has been a Christian. Don't allow the devil to set up this playground in your mind to make you think that you are not worthy because you have just become a Christian or that you are too old. The devil uses this to keep people back from what God has called you do. See, a Christian can be saved for fifty years and not yet be mature. I have known people to be in the church for 20- plus years and they still act like little children when it comes to spiritual things.

The reason why so many people in the church today are still acting like little children is because they are allowing the devil to set up his playgrounds within their minds and keep them back from spiritual growth. As Christians we must grow and mature in the Lord. This is where the enemy would love to set us up with his playground to stunt our growth with the Lord and keep us as a little children. Don't allow it. This reminds me of a sticker that says, "I may be getting older, but I refuse to grow up." A lot of people may grow older but that does not mean that they have grown up. We have to allow the Lord to teach us and show us, and then we will grow and mature into that man/woman that God wants us to be. Don't allow the enemy to try and tell you anything different. For you can have the victory in Jesus in this area.

Maturity has nothing to do with how you looks on the outside. There are a lot of people that look mature, act more spiritual than we do and they have a dignified look about them. They appear to be holy but on the inside they are still immature. Anyone can look spiritual and holy when they want to. Don't allow the devil to set you up with his playground within your mind that you are deceiving others. Become all that God wants you to be and that is to mature in Him.

And maturity has nothing to do with our accomplishments. Just because a person has accomplished a lot in life does not mean that they are mature. The fact is most of those who have accomplished a lot and are successful in life are not even Christian people. Maturity has nothing to do with how much you know or the level of education that you have obtained. Because there are many Christians in the church that have received a PhD {and this does not stand for Pentecostal Hair Do!} and they still live like little children when it comes to their faith in the Lord. We must mature in the Lord and grow into what He wants us to be.

Maturity has everything to do with the Lord.

Maturity is more of an attitude of the mind. It's your attitude that makes the difference in the level of your maturity. Your attitude determines your altitude. Your outlook determines your outcome. What do you determine to do with your mind? Do you determine to listen to the Lord and grow and mature? Or do you determine to let the devil set up his playgrounds within your mind and destroy your maturity and growth in the Lord? It all starts within the mind and we must not allow the enemy to hinder our walk and growth in the Lord by his playgrounds of the mind.

Our attitude is the reflection of our character. Character is who and what we are in the dark when no one else is around to watch us, except God. Reputation is what people think about us based upon what they know about us. Character is what our God says about us because God knows the hidden secrets of our heart. And God is not deceived by our actions when others are watching us. God sees us clearly when there is no one else around and that, my friends, is what God calls our character. It's our attitude that will determine whether we mature or not. God wants us all to grow up and be like the Lord Jesus Christ so that we can reveal a Christ-like attitude in our lives before this lost and dying world. So let's grow up and be more like Jesus every day and not allow the devil to set up his playgrounds within our minds, so that we will not be more like Jesus.

As I carry you through this chapter and as we look in the book of James, we will see signs throughout the book that will indicate to us how far we are from our destination of maturity or how close we are to reaching it. The Bible, God's word, is the manual or road map that will show us how to reach maturity in our lives. We need to consult on God's road map daily to get an idea of where we are in our journey to maturity in God. The word "mature" in Greek is the word "teleaos"---it's translated "mature, complete, perfect." James will show us the journey we must take to become mature in the Lord and in our minds. We measure our spiritual maturity by comparing ourselves to the word of God not by comparing ourselves to others.

James shows us five signs of maturity.

1. The first sign of maturity is the ability to remain positive under pressure.

James 1: 2-4, "My brethren, count it all joy when ye fall into divers temptations; Knowing this, that the trying of your faith works patience. But let patience have her perfect work, that ye may be perfect and entire, wanting nothing." We need to ask ourselves, "How well do I tend to handle pressure? It's how well we respond to pressure and react to pressure. There was a lot of pressure put on the early Christians. They could feel the pressure of troubles, trials and tribulation. They could feel the pressure of temptation to sin. It would appear from James that these Christians weren't responding all that well under the pressure. It appears they were being overwhelmed and overcome by them.

We must not allow the devil to set up his playgrounds of doubt and fear within our minds where we are overcome and overwhelmed by the pressure of life. Because there will be times in our lives that pressure will surround us and we need to be strong so that the enemy will not have a playground to set up within us. For when I am weak Jesus makes me strong. We have the victory in Jesus.

We all live under a certain amount of pressure. And sometimes in our lives the pressure can be overwhelming. But the question is… "How well do we handle ourselves under pressure? Are we blown away by it? Do we get uptight and nervous about it? Do we grumble, complain and gripe about it? My friends, this is just what the devil wants to set us up for in our minds to get us off of what Jesus wants us to do. Don't allow it! As Christians we need to face pressure with a calm assurance of knowing that God is in control and He will not allow anything to come our way that we cannot handle in His strength.

My friends, every believer can live a Christian life when there is no pressure being put on them. But only those that are growing and maturing in their faith and relationship with the Lord Jesus Christ will hold up well under pressure. Those who fail to grow and mature will crumble and fall apart under pressure because they are more concerned about their comfort than their character.

As Christians we need to realize that God is more interested in our character, than He is our comfort zone. I am not saying that God doesn't care about our problems! He most certainly does care! Only that God wants to use the pressure of our problems to develop our character in us for His glory and for our good ultimately. When we feel the pressure of problems bearing down on us, we need to maintain a positive attitude. I know that may sound easier than it is to be done. But we can do all things if we do them through the strength of our Lord and Savior Jesus Christ!

Christianity is more than just a religion. It is a "lifestyle"! It is to be lived out in a loving and living relationship with our Lord Jesus Christ. Jesus said in the word of God, "I've come that you might have life and have it more abundantly than before" {My paraphrasing}. Our life is going to have problems come up from time to time. But life is just that… having problems and solving those problems with the help of our Lord Jesus Christ. Glory to God! And we need to face these problems with a Christ-like attitude. The enemy can set up his playground within our mind if we allow him to concerning this area. Let the enemy know that you will not allow him to hinder you another second because you do have the victory over your problems and pressures in life through Jesus. And to God be all the glory!

And… if you will be honest with yourself… the first thing that your flesh wants to do is RUN. You want to get outta Dodge! But if you run, you will short circuit what God is trying to accomplish in your life for your ultimate good. That is just what the devil would love for you to give into. If you are not careful, the enemy will set up his playground within your mind to cause you to run from God and what the good Lord wants to do for you in your life. God wants to develop a Christ-like character in our lives and the only way that will happen is if we stay put and maintain an attitude of faith and assurance in God's ability to take our pressures and produce within us the qualities that reflect His work and glory. The signs that you are maturing is your willingness to stay put under the pressure and allow God to finish His work in us to our ultimate good in Him.

Look at what James said about those that endure to the end. James 1:12, "Blessed is the man that endures temptation: for when he is tried, he shall receive the crown of life, which the Lord promised to them that love him." We CAN make it!! We have the power within us!! For greater is my God that is within me than he {the devil} who is in the world!!! Give God praise and glory for the victory that you have through Him to endure until the end and then you will receive the crown of life God has promised.

2. The second sign of maturing is being sensitive and loving towards others.

James 2:8 says, "If ye fulfill the royal law according to scripture, Thou shall love thy neighbor as thyself, ye do well." Did you know that it is easy for us to become insensitive toward others when we are feeling the pressure of our problems. It is so easy for us to be lost in our own little world and forget that there are other people around us who are experiencing some of the same pressures. Their problems may vary or

96

be different but the pressure is still just as real. If we are not careful, we can have our own pity party and become insensitive in life. If we don't deal with our problems properly, they can harden us against the needs and pains of others around us. And this is just what the enemy would love to set up in our mind and heart, so that we will be no good to other people around us that are hurting and need our help.

Young Christians that are trying to grow and mature can be very sensitive. Immature Christians at times can be very insensitive towards others. A Christian that is mature, doesn't just see their own needs, they see the needs of others. They are sensitive to their heartaches and pains. They see their needs and they seek for the opportunity and a way to minister to those needs of others. They don't allow the devil to set them up in order to keep them back from really helping those that are in need..... even when they themselves are going through some problems of their own. See, as Christians, if we don't keep a guard on our minds we can show our immaturity when we become self-centered and unconcerned about others.

Look at what James has to say about how we treat others. James 2:1-6, basically says to us, we must not show favoritism and act like a snob by looking down on people. We must not insult them and judge them by appearance. Maturity is also being sensitive and loving towards others...PERIOD! You need to ask yourself this question, "How do I treat other people? Do I treat them like I want to be treated and as the Lord would treat them? Or do I allow the devil to set up his playground within my minds and treat them the way that he wants me to treat them?" We must not allow the enemy to set us up.

1 John 3:17 says, "But whoso hath this world's good, and sees his brother have need, and shuts up his bowels of compassion from him, how dwells the love of God in him?" This word of the Lord is asking us, " How can the love of God dwell in us if we close off our compassion, love and mercy towards those in need?" It can't!! Period!! Saints of God, we must help people when they are hurting and in pain!! We need to open our heart's door with love and minister to them to the best of our ability in the Lord. For if we have not love, we are as sounding brass and as tinkling cymbals the Lord says in His word. It just doesn't amount to much in the sight of our Lord.

3.We need to learn to master our mouth if we are to mature.

James 3:2 says, "For in many things we offend all. If any man offend not in word, the same is a perfect man, and able also to bridle the whole body." This is the third sign of maturity: learning to tame the tongue and mastering the mouth. We need to pray as the Psalmist did in Psalms 141:3, "Set a watch, O Lord, before my mouth; keep the door of my lips." We need to watch out in this area! Because the devil would love to set up his playground within our mind so that we will not even care what comes out of our mouth to hurt people and the ones we love. Don't allow it! Stop it dead {D.O.A} in it's tracks.

We have all been to the doctor and the first thing the doctor says is, "Stick out your tongue and say... "AHHHH!" The doctor uses our tongue to start to check out our health. And our God does the same thing to determine our spiritual health. "Loose lips sink ships," as the old saying goes. Well, loose lips can destroy lives. Your words are very powerful. They can help build a person up or they can tear a person down. They can produce life or they can produce death. Once we speak a word from our lips it can not be stopped. It's like shooting a gun, when the trigger is pulled the powder will ignite and the bullet is on it's way...BANG!... you can't stop it. Much of the trouble that we get ourselves into is a result of what we say. Don't allow the enemy to set you up with his playground within your mind so that you will use your mouth as a tool for the enemy.

James gives us several illustrations in Chapter 3 about the power of the tongue. As I have said earlier in this book, the tongue is like a bit in a horse's mouth. You can put that tiny bit in the horse's mouth and that little bit can control which direction that the powerful horse will go. It's like a tiny spark. One little spark can start a huge forest fire that is out of control. It's like a bite of a deadly snake. One bite and it's deadly. James says your tongue, which, by size is the smallest member of the body... yet it has the power to build up a person or tear down a person. It can be constructive or destructive depending on how you use it. And it has the power to control our life. What you say directs your life. And what we say can destroy your life. It can delight people's lives, or it can discourage people's lives. Our tongue is a powerful force for good or for evil. And we must not allow the enemy to set us up in our minds so that we will use our tongue for the wrong reason. If you are not building up with your words than you are tearing down with them...PERIOD!

Again, we all have heard people say things like, "I just say what's on my mind." And they are proud of it. They just say what's on their mind. Here's a thought...maybe what's on their mind shouldn't even be heard! The Bible says, that's not frankness, that's just immaturity! And that is not of God... it is of the devil. We must not allow it! For all it is, is a playground that the devil has set you up within you that you have got to tear down, my friend.

Ephesians 4:29, "Let no communication proceed out of your mouth, but that which is good to the use of edifying {building up}, that it may minister grace unto the hearers." As Christians we need to say things that "build up" other people. If it doesn't build up someone else... don't even say it. Even if it is the truth. If it doesn't build up... don't even say it. That's a mark of maturity. A mature person manages his or her mouth. It does not matter how long you have been a Christian, if you can't master your mouth, you have missed the mark. And that is just what the devil would love... for you and I to not be able to master the way we use our mouth. So as Christians we need so very much to stay on watch over this area and not allow it to slip in.

James 1:26 says, "If any man among you seems to be religious and bridles not his tongue, but deceives his own heart, this man's religion is vain." Let me say this... you can memorize a hundred verses and have read through the bible over and over and over again, studying it and go to church and never miss a service, etc., but if we can not control our tongue, our religion is worthless, useless, vain and void. PERIOD! We need to speak the truth in love, speak with the right attitude and with the right motive. The Bible is very practical. It does not matter how much you know about the Bible, if our attitude isn't like the Lord Jesus Christ's, we're missing the point. Do not allow the devil to set up his playground in our minds so that we will cause hurt to one another with our tongue.

4. We need to become peacemakers and not troublemakers... this is also another a sign of maturity.

James 4:1 says, "From whence come wars and fights among you? Come they not hence, even of your lusts that war in your members?" In this verse, James is talking about conflict. James is saying quarreling and fighting that is going on in the church is a result of our inner {lusts} desires. You want something that you don't have and you can't get it. So you end up destroying one another in order to get it. And that is a playground that the devil has set up in your mind to make you think that's it's ok to do this type of thing among your fellow Christians. But the truth of the matter is, that it is not ok and it is not of God and it will destroy someone's life and valuable friendships. So we must not allow the enemy to set his playground of selfish lusts within our minds so that they will not enter our hearts and then come out of our mouths to hurt and destroy people.

In the Book of Matthew 5:9 it says, "Blessed are the peacemakers: for they shall be called the children of God." You need so very much to ask yourself, "Am I a troublemaker or am I a peacemaker? Am I a contentious person? Do I hurt other people's feelings? Do I like to argue? Do I get my feelings hurt as well?" Remember what I said before in this book, hurting people hurt others. The devil does not want you to become a peacemaker. If the enemy can set up any kind of playground within your mind to keep you back from becoming a peacemaker he will. So it is up to you, as a Christian, to not allow the devil to do so. For you can have the victory in Jesus our Lord in this area.

Becoming a peacemaker for the Lord's glory is exhibiting {showing} to the world that we are children of the Most High God. And this will be due to the fact that we ourselves have inner peace in God. A peacemaker is one that is always looking for peace and having peace with others rather than looking to see where they can stir up trouble. A sure sign of a mature Christian is the lack of conflicts in his/her own life with others. Paul told the Corinthian church, "you people are like babies. You argue about everything!" {my paraphrasing}. They argued about the Lord's supper, gifts, leadership,.... Everything possible under the sun and beyond! And that is a mark of immaturity. Let's not allow the devil to put a playground of immaturity within our minds.

As Christians we should be the most easiest people in this world to get along with. I am not saying that you and I are to be doormats for everyone to step on and wipe their feet upon or to be pushed around. But we should not go looking around for trouble nor should we throw a temper tantrum when things just don't seem to go our way or we don't get everything we want. For a true peacemaker is a person that has learned to be happy and content with what they have until God provides more or better. For if you are faithful in the little, God will bless you with much more.

And then James goes on to say there are two reasons for conflict. James 4:3, "Ye ask, and receive not, because ye ask amiss, that ye may consume it upon your lust." Here we see the first cause of conflict is selfishness. When you want what you want constantly then inevitably we are going to have conflict with somebody. The playground is pride. You must not allow the devil to set up his playground of pride within our mind and heart. "Pride cometh before the fall" as the word of God states in the book of Proverbs. And that is just what the enemy would love for you to do....fall! Fall flat on your face in the mud! SPLAT!! While the enemy is laughing at you off at a safe distance.

Now look at what James says in verse 11-12, "Speak not evil one of another, brethren. He that speaks evil of his brother, and judges his brother, speaks evil of the law {God's Holy Word}. And judges the law: but if thou judge the law, thou art not a doer of the law, but a judge.

There is one lawgiver, who is able to save and to destroy: who art thou that judges another." Now we can see the other source of conflict is "judging others"---being judgmental. And at times all of us have been guilty of being judgmental. God says don't judge people. If you do so, you are asking for a fight from all directions. We should not be fault-finders...always finding fault in someone or something. Always stirring up strife. Always spreading rumors. Let's not allow the enemy to set up his playground within our mind so that we will start being judgmental towards others. God's telling us through His word that we are not to judge.

As peacemakers we are not to go around judging other people.... PERIOD! Why? Well, let's look at three reasons why we are not to judge.

A. We are not God! {For a real good starter!}

When we start judging people, we are playing the role of God. And that is a big, big, big, big mistake! There is only one judge, only one lawgiver----GOD! Don't allow the devil to set you up to where you start trying to "help" God. For one thing, God doesn't need our help when it comes to being "THE JUDGE" over all the earth. That's God's job...not ours'!! Don't allow the enemy to set up this lie within you.

B. God has ALL of the facts, we don't!

We can start judging and we don't know all the facts. If we judge someone, we are judging them with the limited knowledge that we have. We don't know what that person has been through. We don't know the problems that others face on a daily bases. We don't know their heart. However, God does know the condition of everyone's heart and life... therefore His judgment is based upon the true facts. God is a true facts kind of God!

C. We don't know their motives.

We can't tell what's in someone else's heart. Only God does. So God has the only right to judge someone. He knows all the facts! God knows everything, He knows all the motives of our hearts. He sees into the heart. He knows the truth so He can judge by that truth for He is God of all creation. But we are limited in our insight. And we don't have the right to judge. So don't allow the devil to place his playground within your mind to make you think that it's ok for you to judge someone, when it's not ok with God. Stop trying to do God's job! God says judgmental people are immature. Be a peacemaker not a troublemaker.

5. Patience and prayer are a sign of maturity.

James 5: 7-8, "Be patient therefore, brethren, unto the coming of the Lord. Behold, the husbandman waited for the precious fruit of the earth, and hath long patience for it, until he receive the early and latter rain. Be ye also patient; establish your hearts: for the coming of the Lord draw's nigh." James 5: 16 says, "Confess your faults one to another, and pray one for another, that ye may be healed. The effectual fervent prayer of a righteous man avails much." These are the key words in chapter five... "Patient" is mentioned five times. "Prayer" is mentioned seven times. So one of the signs of a mature Christian is that they are prayerful and patient. These two go together. They express an attitude of dependence upon our God the Father.

James gives us an illustration of a farmer to describe patience. Farmers they have to wait and they have to be very patient people. They have to do a lot of waiting. They plant the seed, they wait, they pray, and hope for a good crop. Just like a farmer has to wait, sometimes you and I have to wait. We have to wait upon God in answer to our prayers. We have to wait on God for a miracle. We have to wait on God to work out things in our lives. The only way you and I can learn patience is by waiting. And God knows this too. We must not allow the devil to set up his playground within our minds and lie to us that what we have been praying about will never be answered. That it has been a long time and that we are not going to get it.... just give up. My friend, tell the devil that you know what he is trying to tell you is a lie from the pits of hell itself and that help IS on the way in Jesus' name!

We must be patient with one another and prayerful for one another. Many times God will tell us, "Not just yet." He doesn't mean, "No." And it doesn't mean that He is not going to answer your prayer. God's timing is all perfect and right on time! God is just saying, "You have to wait with patience. I want you to develop patience and to grow. I just want you to mature, My child." Let's learn to wait upon the Lord, my friend. Don't allow the enemy to place his playground of impatience within you, but learn to wait upon God for He will bring you through to victory. Just give him praise for the victory and the answers to your prayers.

What are the tests?

1. How you handle your problems?
   Do you get uptight, negative, grumble, gripe, and complain? Or are you positive under pressure and with patience wait upon the Lord's timing?

2. Are you extra-sensitive to other people?
    Are you concerned about their needs, hurts, cares, and desires or do you only see yourself? Do you only pray about your needs and not pray for others?
3. Can you manage your mouth?
    Have you learned to put a muzzle on it and just say nothing?
4. Do you tend to be a troublemaker or a peacemaker?
    Do you have a tendency to stir up things? Do you carry a grudge? Do you find yourself nursing old bitterness? Or are you a peacemaker?
5. How long do you wait for an answer to prayer without giving up?

God may have every intention of giving it to you, but He's waiting to teach you some patience in your growth in Him to help you mature.

Let me ask you this: Are you a believer in Jesus Christ? Are any of these signs missing from your life? What playgrounds has the devil set up within your mind that you need to tear down in order to mature in the Lord? Where do you need to become Christ-like? Don't allow another day, another second, another minute, to pass by that you allow the enemy to keep his playgrounds within your mind to keep you back from spiritual maturity. Tear them down! In Jesus' name! For you have the victory in Jesus.

Chapter Twelve:
The Power You Get When
You Have A Made Up Mind

Joshua 24: 14-15 says, "Now therefore fear the Lord, and serve him in sincerity and in truth: and put away the gods which your fathers served on the other side of the flood, and in Egypt; and serve ye the Lord. And if it seem evil unto you to serve the Lord, choose you this day whom ye will serve; whether the gods which your fathers served that were on the other side of the flood, or the gods of the Amorites, in whose land ye dwell: as for me and my house, we will serve the Lord."

I would like to tell you about one of the greatest powers on the face of this earth. It is a power that you can possess as a Christian. I just want to draw your attention to it, because it is a power that God wants you and I to execute. I would like to talk to you about THE POWER OF A MADE UP MIND. Everything that happens in our lives comes from our mind… good or bad. This is why we cannot allow the devil to set up his playground within our minds. And before it came from the minds of men… it first came from the mind of God.

And when it comes down to you and I, everything we see came out of the mind. Every single automobile, etc., every physical, tangible thing that we can see and touch man has made came from the mind. First, it is conceived in our mind from the Lord then birthed out of us. The mind is one of the most powerful forces that you and I have to utilize. God is saying to many that is reading this book, "I want you to make up your mind." And whatever area that you sense God dealing with you in, make up your mind to do it. Don't allow the devil to keep you back from doing it. For the enemy would love to set up his playground within your mind to keep you back from where God wants to take you this day. Don't allow it.

My friends, I want to give you something that will help you. I would like to lay a tool in your hands that will help you accomplish what God wants you to accomplish. And it's all preceded by a made up mind. Have you ever asked a person that you admired, "How did you accomplish that?" And they will tell you that they had "a made up mind" to do it. And that's just what the Lord wants from us, is a made up mind to serve Him and He will lead you and I in the right directions. God may want you to invent something, write something, etc., someday and, if you don't have a made up mind to do it, you may lose out on His blessings. Don't allow the enemy to set you up within your mind to distract you from serving the Lord and receiving what He has for you. Have a made up mind to do your best for God and He will do His best for you.

In your life you will have to have a made up mind. You will have to choose in whom you will serve. And even if I try to inspire you through this book to not allow the enemy to set up his playgrounds within your mind, YOU will still have the choice to listen or not. It's up to you to make up your own mind. But my friend, it will be awesome what that you will be able to do and accomplish for God if you will make up your mind to do it God's way. Take back what the enemy is trying to steal from you. Amen!

You may be thinking: "Why is it so necessary for me to make up my mind?"

1. If you want the victory in areas in your life that you need victory in it's preceded by a made up mind.

How are you going to get the victory over fear? How are you going to get the victory over lust? For some their worst problem is their temper. They are very hot tempered and it's not because they heritage either! I've heard people say, "I have a hot temper because I'm Irish", or "German," etc. That is not it! They are just hot tempered PERIOD!! How are you going to get the victory over anger? How are you going to get over these areas in your life that you know that are there? Let me tell you how you will get the victory. It is having a made up mind! With that you can have the victory in any area of your life that you are struggling with. You cannot allow the devil to set you up with a playground of defeat within your mind.

We have to make up our minds this day! You have to be tired of giving into the playground of fear that the devil sets up within your mind. Speak this out loud and from your heart: "I am tired of it, tired of worrying. Tired of the enemy setting up his playground of doubting God within my mind. I am tired of all this confusion that the enemy is using as a playground within my mind. And I have made up my mind that I will not allow the devil another day to set his playground up in any area of my life. For I have the victory in Jesus over all these areas. Praise God for the victory. I am going to trust my God! I am going to believe God! Victory in Jesus is just what I have."

2.Nothing changes externally {outside} until it changes internally {inside}.

What does it mean nothing will change externally until it changes internally? It means that your problem is not going to go away until you change on the inside first. Some would say, "If I will just give it enough time it will get better." But "time" is not your friend. You may be thinking, "What are you saying?" I am saying, nothing is going to change externally {on the outside} until it changes internally {on the inside}. If you are having trouble in your marriage, it will not get any better until you make up your mind to do something about it on your part to make it better. And you will not get out of debt until you make up your mind to get out of debt. Change how you think about finances, etc. It will not go away until you do. Nothing will change externally until it changes internally. It is birthed in your mind. You have to make up your mind that you are going to do something about the issue. And not allow the devil to use your mind as his playground. Resist the enemy and he will have to take up his playground and leave.

My friends, you are in limbo until you do. And that is the worse place you could be and it's the place the devil would have you to be. He would love to set up your mind and life in limbo, one of his playgrounds. And do you know why? Because you have been neutralized! See, Satan does not want you to go forward. He just wants you in neutral. You don't know whether to go, whether to stay. "Should I?" Should I not?" "Should I?" "Should I?" I'm not sure?" Should I, could I, would I... they don't mean a hill of beans when it comes down to it. It is a frustrating place to be. But you will stay there until you make up your own mind. And then once you have made up your mind this helps you set everything into motion. You don't allow the devil to use your mind any longer as his playground to keep you back.

Once that you have made up your mind, you then become like a magnet and you draw your mind upon the things of God that are necessary to help you make the right decisions within your mind and life. And then all the people that will come into your life will help you to keep this fervent mindset that God wants you to be in. And then, my friend, once that you have made up your mind for the good of doing what God wants for your life and mind, all of the things that you begin to draw to yourself will be the things that will help you, encourage you and strengthen you in the areas that you have made up your mind to correct.

I am telling you friends, that if you make up your mind to do the things of God and not allow the devil to place his playgrounds within your mind, just watch the wonderful things that will gravitate to you. Praise God for the victory in Jesus. God is saying to many that is reading this book, "I want you to make up your mind so that I can use you greatly in my work and bless you in the process."

"Just how do I make up my mind?" You have to first seize the moment of opportunity. And the moment of opportunity is just this. There will be a time, in time itself, where there is no better time than that time for you to make up your mind. You will recognize it if you really have made up your mind. Listen, seize the moment of opportunity. Be led by God's Holy Spirit. God wants you to make up your mind. You are not in this by yourself either. See, God does grieve {hurts} when problems come upon us that the devil tries to defeat us with through our mind. So the very things that you are trying to get the victory over is the very things that God wants you to get victory over. Don't allow the devil to set your mind up with his playgrounds of defeat so that you will be no good for God's work. For God gave you the victory through his Son Jesus Christ.

God will create and God will send a season, a moment and a time that is perfect. God may be talking to you at this time to seize this moment. "This is the moment I created just for you," God may be trying to tell you. God is saying, "For behold I stand at the door and knock and all I want from you is for you to jump on it now. Because the longer you wait and the longer you put something off, the more of the impact and importance it will lose." Joshua said, "Choose you this day." In other words, "make up your mind right now." And that is what God is saying to a lot of you that is reading this book. Make up your mind right now that you are going to forgive that person who hurt you. Don't allow the enemy to keep you back another day without forgiving them. Make up your mind that you are going to live right for God, come hell or high water, come good times, bad times or sad times. Don't allow the devil to place playgrounds within your mind and life to keep you back from what God wants to do in you.

You need to shout it out!! "As for me and my house, we are going to serve the Lord! I have made up my mind!. Praise the Lord!" Seize this moment of opportunity. For the moment of opportunity is the best time "in time." It's the time when there is no better time than at this time to do what God wants you to do. Seize the moment of opportunity.

Also capitalize on being frustrated with your frustration. Now why did I just say that? Because a lot of people waste their frustration. You may be thinking, "What in the world are you talking about preacher?" They are frustrated, but they don't let their frustrations motivate them to do something positive about it. It's like they just want to stay frustrated. Like they are stuck being frustrated. "Yes, I am frustrated. I was frustrated last week. I will be frustrated next week." Are you going to do anything about it? "No, I'm just frustrated!" You are going to have to do something with your frustration! Let your frustration motivate you! Don't allow the devil to keep setting up your mind with his playgrounds of frustrations. Motivate your self in the midst of your frustration and allow the Lord to help you in all things. For you have the victory in Jesus.

God used a man name Paul to preach to the Gentiles. Do you know what led Paul to preach to the Gentiles? His frustration with the Jews for not listening to the Gospel! So his frustration became a motivating factor to do something for the glory of God! What are you doing about your frustration? Is your frustration becoming a motivating factor to do something for the Lord? Don't allow the enemy to stop you from turning your frustration into a motivating factor to be used of the Lord.

We must focus on accomplishing just one thing at a time. "One thing have I desired of the Lord," Psalm 27:4. Not two or three things. People have needs they pray about like: "God help me financially, God heal my marriage, God I need a new car, and God I need new clothes, You are in the giving business!" But we need to say sometimes, "There is one thing that I want you to do for me, God, and I am focused on that one thing." See, God is not asking you to make up your mind in 50 different ways. Just keep it simple. God is just saying for you to make up your mind in one area {and you know that area because it is a frustrating area}." It is an area that nags you. Let me say that all of us are trying to be right before the Lord. But it can become frustrating when you are trying to get too many things done right. And that is just what the devil would like to use as a playground within your mind so that you will become so burdened down and frustrated that you are no good to anyone and not good for God. Don't allow it to take place.

Christianity is not using your strength to live a godly life… it's God desiring to live out His character in us. You will become frustrated if you try to be godly, because you can't be godly in your own strength. Oh, you may be able to hang in there for a while, and then the real you is going to surface… the carnal {fleshly} person. Christianity is the desire of God to live his life in you. That is why it is so unique. There is nothing like Christianity. Religion is mankind trying to get to God. Christianity is God trying to get to mankind. We should yield ourselves unto God totally! Praise the Lord! God wants all of us or none of us! Focus on just one thing at a time to mature in and don't allow the devil just to use your mind as his playground and try and make you focus on too many things at once that will keep you from going forward with the Lord. For that is the enemies goal… to distract you.

We must stand fast in the moment of challenges. Whatever you make up your mind to do, something or someone will challenge you in it. Have you ever noticed that whenever you have made up your mind to fast, ten people will invite you to lunch. UGH!! You made up your mind to do something and something will come along to challenge it. So then and there you have to stand fast in the moment of challenge. Say, "No!" I have made up my mind! Stand fast!

Don't be afraid to ask God for help. Philippians 4:13, "I can do all things through Christ which strengthens me." Listen, my friends, always tap into the Lord's strength for everything that you need or want. Everything you desire that is good comes from Christ who lives in you if you are born again in Jesus Christ. Those good desires come from He who lives in us. So when you're tapping into the Lord who lives within you, something awesome is bound to happen. You are empowered to do something that you did not have the ability to do on your own. Why? Because Jesus lives inside of you and all His power comes with Him to dwell there inside of you as well. You can love somebody that you didn't love at first. And you can forgive somebody and mean it. Don't allow another day to past that the devil will keep his playgrounds within your mind to keep you back from receiving what God has for you this day. For we have the victory in Jesus.

Chapter Thirteen:
You Must Keep A Made Up Mind

Hebrews 11: 24-27, "By faith Moses, when he was come to years, refused to be called the son of Pharaoh's daughter: Choosing rather to suffer affliction with the people of God, than enjoy the pleasures of sin for a season; Esteeming the reproach of Christ greater riches than the treasures in Egypt: for he had respect unto the recompense of the reward. By faith he forsook Egypt, not fearing the wrath of the king: for he endured, as seeing him who is invisible."

In this chapter we will go into how you must "keep" a made up mind in the Lord. If not, the enemy will come with his playground of deceptions within your mind to try and destroy you and your work for God. It is one thing to make up your mind and it's another thing to "keep" your mind made up. So not only does God want you to make up your mind, but God wants you to keep your mind made up. And there are a lot of people who make up their mind and somewhere along the line they blow it! They didn't go all the way to the end! What happened? They didn't keep their mind made up. They allowed the devil to set them up in their minds and thus blew the opportunity to keep their mind made up. We must stay focused on the things of God.

And not only does God want you to make up your mind to be a man or woman of God, but that we will let the past go. That we are going to forgive people, that we are going to be a better husband, a better wife, etc., that we are going to get out of debt and stay out of it, that we are going to stop lying and deceiving, that we are going to be all that our Lord wants us to be. God wants us to keep our minds made up! God not only wants us to make up our minds, but He wants us to stay focused! It's one thing for us to start the race, but it's another thing to finish the race. And God wants us to become a winner. We must stop the enemy from placing his playground within our mind and keeping us back from becoming winners in God's race.

God wants you to become a winner in the tough areas of your life. But the enemy will try his best to keep you back and you must not allow this to happen to you. God does not want you to be depressed all the time but the devil does. God does not want you frustrated all the time but the enemy does. God does not want you feeling sorry for yourself all the time but the devil does. All these are playgrounds that the devil would love to set up within your mind if he hasn't already done so in you. Don't allow the devil to do it to you. For God wants you to stand up in your spirit! There are many who are reading this book that God is saying to you… "Stand up! I want you to stand up!"

Some of you who are reading this book have Jesus within you, but you are trying to keep Him in a box. He's limited by your way of thinking. He's limited by your mindset, your frustrations, your fears and anxieties. All in which are playgrounds of the enemy. But Jesus wants to burst loose on the inside you. We are not trying to get God from within us; we should let God loose on the inside! See, He is already in us and he wants to manifest Himself inside totally, so we can be what we are supposed to be for His glory! So you and I need to be praying and asking God to help us not to just make up our minds, but to keep our minds made up.

I would like to show you through certain biblical men of God, who had a made up mind and didn't allow the devil to set them up with playgrounds within their minds to keep them back from what God called them to do.

The first man is Moses. Hebrews 11: 24 says, "By faith Moses, when he was come to years, refused to be called the son of Pharaoh's daughter." You can see encased in this verse a man who had a made up mind. When he had gotten to a certain age, he wanted nothing more to do with Egypt. From that point on he made up his mind, he didn't want anything to do with the world. He would turn his back on the world. And that is just what we should do as well and not allow the enemy to place anything different within our minds. I can hear Moses shouting this, "For me and my house we will serve the Lord." He turned his attention to the things of God. And so in essence, Moses had a made up mind.

But just how did Moses keep his mind made up?

Hebrews 11;25-27 says, "Choosing rather to suffer affliction with the people of God, than to enjoy the pleasures of sin for a season: Esteeming the reproach of Christ greater riches than the treasures in Egypt: for he had respect unto recompense of the reward. By faith he forsook Egypt, not fearing the wrath of the king; for he endured, as seeing him who is invisible." The thing that kept his mind made up is he kept looking to God and didn't allow the devil to set his mind up with his playground devices. Moses kept seeing the invisible. There is an inner sight that you and I have with in us, and sometimes we see through it and sometimes we don't. But hear me , there is an inner sight in you and I and it is the eyes of faith. It is the ability to see that which is invisible! Faith is seeing that which is not, and seeing that which is. Moses endured, he was able to keep his focus, he was able to hang in there, because he was able to see Him who is invisible. His attention was focused on the things of God. You and I must not allow the devil to set up his playground within our minds so that we will not stay focused on the things that God has called us to do.

How do we learn to "keep" our minds made up? You must continue to hold in your mind the picture of what you are trying to get accomplished for the Lord. Don't lose that vision. Just what is it that you are seeing? Moses wanted to be a man of God, so he sees God. That was what kept him. You have to see through your spiritual eyes a picture of just what you are trying to accomplish in life. Are you trying to get closer to God? Then read and study the word, pray daily and don't allow the devil to set up his playground within your mind to get you sidetracked in not doing these important things. Whatever you are trying to accomplish, you have to see it. Can you see yourself in a new home? Can you see yourself with a new job, with more pay? Can you see yourself in a new car? Can you sit down and visualize it? I am not talking about fantasies here people. I am talking about faith sight. I am talking about seeing something in your spiritual sight. Don't allow the devil to steal this away from you by placing his playgrounds of doubt and fear within you.

Just what are you seeing? What is going to keep your mind made up? Can you see yourself as a good wife? Can you see yourself as a good husband? Can you see yourself executing what is necessary on your job? Can you see yourself driving that new car? Can you see yourself in that new home? Moses endured by seeing Him {God} who is invisible. And if we do the same the Lord will be with us to the point that we see things come to past that we have been longing to see come to reality in our lives. Don't allow the devil to set you up with his playground of lies and deceptions because that is just what he wants to do so he can keep you from the blessings of God. Believe me, God does want so very much to bless us!

Let's look at another man by the name of Joseph. Genesis 39: 7-9, "And it came to pass after these things, that his master's wife cast her eyes upon Joseph; and she said, Lie with me. But he refused, and said unto his master's wife, Behold, my master wotteth not what is with me in the house, and he hath committed all that he hath to my hand; There is none greater in this house than I; neither hath he kept back any thing from me but thee, because thou art his wife;: how then can I do this great wickedness, and sin against God?"

Now we see a woman that wants to have an affair with Joseph, but we can sense in his tone....he is a person that has made up his mind to serve God and not allow the enemy to set him up. You can sense a person who has a made up mind to serve the Lord. They are not going to have an affair with someone who is not their spouse. Joseph was a person who had a made up mind. "I will not do that which is wrong in God's eyes," Joseph said. And we can have a made up mind to do what God wants you and I to do and not allow the devil to set up his playground within our minds to make us sin and not reap the true blessings of God.

Genesis 39: 9-10 (NIV) says, "How then could I do such a wicked thing and sin against God?" And though she spoke to Joseph day after day, he refused to go to bed with her or even be around her by himself. Very wise young man!

Notice that if you don't resist the devil and his playgrounds day after day you will give into that sin. Don't allow this to take place in your mind. Because whatever you have victory over today is going to keep knocking at your door and trying to get in. Day after day, it's going to come back. You said, "No!" to something that you knew was wrong Monday and you will most likely have to say, "No!" to it again come Tuesday. You will be tried and tempted, Saints of God, as you mature in the Lord. You might have to say, "No!" three to a hundred times on Tuesday, then on Wednesday morning you may have to say, "No!" again. See, we are talking about "keeping" a made up mind. I made up my mind to serve the Lord when I got saved! I wasn't playing around! "But what about now?", you may ask. Now I have to "keep" my mind made up. I refuse to go back to where I was saved out of. Yes, the temptations come but I "keep" a made up mind to serve the Lord every day of my life! So I rebuke and send the devil packing in Jesus' name! The devil will flee because I submit myself before God daily and I stay humble, I never forget where Jesus brought me out of! I choose to keep that made up mind! We must not allow the devil to use our mind as his playground because the enemy WILL try us each day. We have to put on the whole armor of God, submit ourselves humbly before THE Living God, resist the devil and he will flee from us. God will break down the playgrounds of the enemy that he is trying to use on us and through our minds.

And one day Joseph went into the house to attend to his daily duties, and none of the household servants were inside. And guess what… she caught him by his cloak and said, "Come lay with me! But Joseph left his cloak in her hand and ran out of the house." Genesis 39:11-14 NIV. "When she had saw that he had left his cloak in her hand and had run out of the house, she called her household servants. Look, she said to them, this Hebrew has been brought to us to make sport of us!" She in essence had framed him, and we know the rest of the story, he ended up incarcerated in prison for something he did not even do. That is just like the devil to try and set us up for things through his deceitful lies, false accusations. And at times he will use our minds as his playground to do so and we must not allow this to take place in our lives as children of the Most High God.

For some of you that are reading this book, God is saying to you, "Learn that a good run is better than a bad stand!" Remember a man named General Armstrong Custer? He had to run from trouble! There is nothing wrong with running when it is appropriate. Sometimes you have to get out of situations or get yourself scalped! If you are in a situation where there is a beautiful woman or a handsome man and the devil is setting you up…RUN!!!… feet had best not fail you! RUN!!! Get outta Dodge, partner! Don't allow yourself to be in that playground of the devil!!!

The scripture says to flee youthful lust. Run far away from it! It is a strong and wise person who knows where they are weak and to not stay in that situation! There are certain weaknesses that people have. Certain areas where they can't go! You have got to run. You have got to leave that tempting den of the devil he is using to set you up for that fall. God wants us to, "Rebuke it and run out of it quickly! Make up your mind and run out from that devilish den! Run to Jesus for He has a place of shelter and rest for you. A place of life, purity, holiness, and righteousness!

We have to keep our eyes upon the Lord. David was a man of God that did just that. He set in front of him things that reminded him of God. Psalm 16:8 NIV… "I have set the Lord always before me, Because he is at my right hand, I will not be shaken." David was saying, "I will not be shaken. I will not be moved. I will be able to keep my mind made up." David was able to make up his mind and keep his mind made up. How ? He set the Lord before him.

What does this mean? They didn't have a cross at that time to look to in the time of David, but they had the word of God, the Torah. He could place his Torah, his Bible, God's Holy Word, in front of him. There was something he could set in front of him to remind him of God. Let me say this: if you are have a problem with seeing things you don't want to see while doing your business on the internet, take your Bible and set it on top of your computer. If you know you are having a problem, take something, like your Bible , and set it on the computer I said. Every time you are on the computer to do your work, you will see a visual reminder of God…His Holy Word. You see, the Holy Spirit will convict you and bring you back to your senses when you see that Bible sitting up on top of your computer. My friends, God is still God and Jesus is still Lord and worthy to be praised! What ever the enemy is trying to use as a playground within your mind to keep you back from receiving the full blessings of God, get ready to let it loose and be set free in Jesus name. Don't allow the devil to trick you one more minute.

As Christians we need to listen to and obey God's will and His way. Just maybe some of you that are reading this book need to do this on your job. Don't be ashamed of the Gospel of Jesus Christ! I am not talking about you wearing a huge cross. But I am talking about your life…showing people that you are a God-fearing man/woman of God. And someone might notice that Light of Jesus you carry on the inside of you shining through to them on the outside of you and ask you what you have or do that makes you who you are? What's it all about? And then you can share with them the love and salvation of the Lord and Savior Jesus Christ, and you are a walking reminder of what Jesus did for all on the cross to those you work around on a daily basis. Even the simplest little pocket New Testament does the same thing when you carry it with you to work and people see the difference in you when you read it on your lunch break, etc. And it keeps your mind clear of the devil's playground toys that he tries to use within your mind on a daily basis.

David said, "I have set the Lord always before me." That word "set" means "equalizer, a counterbalance, something to keep me or help me maintain composure." I have set an equalizer, a counterbalance, in front of me. I have set something before me that will help me maintain my composure. So you set your Bible someplace. Why? Because it is a counterbalance. And when the enemy tries to put his playgrounds within your mind to stop you from doing the work that God has called you to do you have a counterbalance and it helps you to keep focused on what God has called you to do. Praise God that you and I have the victory in Jesus.

Another way for you to keep your mind made up is to learn to run with the good runners. Hebrews 12:1 NIV, "Therefore, since we are surrounded by such a great cloud of witnesses, let us throw off everything that hinders and the sin that so easily entangles, and let us run with perseverance the race marked out for us."

We are running a race. What does that mean? There are people all around us that love God with all their heart, soul, mind and strength. There are people who are full of God. There are people who are God-oriented. And what God wants you to do is hook up, associate yourself with somebody that is running for the glory of God! We need to be connected with God. One thing that you need to learn is to be connected and surround by godly runners. And don't allow the devil to put his playground thoughts within your mind to keep you back from the fellowship of the saints that are truly runners for God. The real "athletes" in God!

God wants us to keep our minds made up for the glory of God. And one of the ways you can do this is to run with a good runner. Run with someone you know that is running with God. You can see God in them and on them. They are God-oriented. Get with them. Link up with them and run with them. Because the best of us, including your pastor, are strong sometimes and then at other times, they may need support, a hand up, to keep from falling. And if you and I run with somebody else, who happens to be a strong and good runner, we can receive help up, so we can get our self squared away again.

Sometimes God will call you to run with someone. And sometimes God will show you someone that is lagging behind. And He will tell us to get with them, run with them and help them. Every once in a while, God will assign you somebody. He will say, "That brother/sister is struggling in their marriage," "their finances" or "health". They have lost their confidence and courage in Me. Now you run with them until they get back on their feet." Yes, the heavenly Father does just that at times! Don't allow the enemy to set up his playgrounds within your mind so that you will not hear from God about helping others that might need your help so they won't fall down. Be open to the voice of

God so that you can help whoever it is to keep running the race that has been set before them in God.

Then another way that we can make up our minds is to reject everything that the devil is using as his playground within our minds to contradict what we have made up our minds to do. In Nehemiah 6:1-3 NIV, we see that Nehemiah made up his mind that they were going to build the walls. Sanballat, Tobiah and Geshem tried to stop him, but he rejected anything contrary to what he had made up his mind to do. You may have made up your mind to lose weight this year. Good for you! But how many know that you will most likely pass by everything on your way to work every morning that is absolutely off of your diet? If you have made up your mind though you can do it through Jesus' strength. You have to reject everything contrary to what you have made up your mind to do. Don't allow the devil to place his playgrounds of defeat and fear within your mind and tell you that you can't… because he is lying to you. For you have the power and you have the victory over the playgrounds of your mind in Jesus name. Go for it!!!

In this chapter, I believe I have told you what God has placed within my heart to tell you. And I pray to the good Lord that I wrote something that would challenge and encourage you that have been reading this book {and this chapter in particular} in a certain area that made you want to keep your mind made up for the things of God. I pray that I have gave you some tool. Something that you can put in your hands, and use to keep your mind made up. And to anoint you and give you the ability to make up your mind and keep your mind made up. And then one day you will hear the Lord say well done thy good and faithful servant enter into the joys of the Lord.

Chapter Fourteen: The Renewed Mind

A Christian life is to be a transformed life....one that does not conform to the things of this world. Romans 12:2(a), "And be not conformed to this world: but be ye transformed by the renewing of your mind." We as Christians can have a renewed mind. We don't have to allow the devil to use our mind as his playground. For our minds can be transformed into the perfect will of God. Don't allow the devil to tell you anything different. In Romans 12:2(b) it seeks to prove or demonstrate that God's way is better. "That ye may prove what is that good, and acceptable, and perfect, will of God."

If you and I as Christians allow God to renew our minds daily we will have no time for the devil to set up his playgrounds within our minds to keep us back from doing what God has called us into for Him. We will start to think like Jesus, act like Jesus, talk like Jesus, walk like Jesus. And we will not fulfill the lust of the flesh. For we will be thinking on the things of Christ and we will become acceptable, good, and do the perfect will of our God.

See, the Christian life requires a renewing of our mind. And the devil is out there to try and stop this in any way that he can. He knows if he can't get you in other areas, he will try through the mind so that you will not focus on the things of God and that your mind will not be renewed. And in the word we learn what is God's will for our mind... Romans 12:2(b). And in return making it possible to be transformed... Romans 12: 2(a). We are to have a renewed mind that we may prove what is that good and acceptable, and perfect will of God.

There are some indications of a renewed mind. For Romans 12:16 says, "Be of the same mind one toward another. Mind not high things, but condescend to men of low estate. Be not wise in your own conceits."

Here we find the mind or attitude that is to be found among us Christians. First, that there is to be......Sameness of mind. What does this mean? In the NKJV it reads, "Be of the same mind towards one another..." Literally thinking the same thing. The Christians in Rome for example...Romans 15:5 says, "Now the God of patience and consolation grant you to be likeminded one toward another according to Jesus." The Christians in Corinth for example...1 Cor. 1:10 says, "Now I beseech you, brethren, by the name of our Lord Jesus Christ, that ye all speak the same thing, and that there be no divisions among you; but that ye be perfectly joined together in the same mind and in the same judgment." The Christians in Philippi for example...Phil. 1:27; 2:2-3; 3:16; 4:2. The Christians in Asia for example... 1 Pet 3 :8 says, "Finally , be ye all of one mind, having compassion one of another, love as brethren, be pitiful, be courteous."

As a child of God we need to follow these examples in the scriptures so that we can and will have a renewed and made up mind for God. We see in these scriptures that the Christians in Rome, Corinth, Philippi, & Asia were likeminded one towards another according to Jesus Christ. They were joined together in the same mind. We as Christians can be likeminded in Jesus Christ our Lord. Don't allow the devil to place a playground within your mind and tell you any different.

As we are renewed in our minds, we will begin having similar goals, aims, views in the body of Christ. You may ask, "How is this possible? We must seek the mind of Christ. Philippians 2:5 says, "Let this mind be in you, which was also in Christ Jesus." Saints of God, each of us should strive to develop and emulate the mindset of Christ. And don't allow the enemy to set you up with his playground of confusion within your mind and tell you that you can't have the mind of Christ. The more we become like Christ the sooner we become of the same mind. You must set your mind on the things above. Colossians 3:1-2 says, "Set your affection on the things above, not on the things on this earth. For you are dead, and your life is hid with Christ in God." We should focus our attention more on spiritual matters for the distractions of worldly matters and human opinions, will destroy our oneness of mind. And where there is no unity, someone is (perhaps most aren't) not setting their mind on Christ and the things above. And this is just where the devil would love to set your mind up with his playground to keep you back from loving your fellow Christians. Don't allow it.

Another indication of a renewed mind is "lowliness of mind". What this means is "do not set your mind on high things (NKJV)". Other translations: "Do not be haughty (RSV)." "Do not be too ambitious (Good-speed)." "Do not aspire to eminence (Berkley)." "Don't become snobbish. (Phillips)." "But we must associate with the humble (NKJV)." "But take a interest in ordinary people (Phillips)." For a renewed mind makes a concerted effort not to be snobbish or ambitious, willing to be associated with humble tasks and lowly people. See, my friends in the Lord, if you are snobbish or ambitious towards others, the enemy has set you up within your mind several of his playgrounds and you need to get them out of your life. Resist the devil and he will flee from your mind and life.

How is it possible to do these things mentioned? Let us look at the word of God again. The attitude of David--Psalm 131:1-2. The warning to Jeremiah--Jeremiah 45:5. The teaching of Jesus--Luke 22:24-27. And also by noting what you and I learn from: The example of Jesus in Philippians 2:5-8. The teaching of James in James 2: 1-5. When we have the mind of Christ, our lowliness of mind will be manifested by the nature of our goals and the company we keep.

And also the renewed mind possesses....humbleness of mind. And what this means is do not be wise in your own opinion. Do not think too highly of yourself. Do not be conceited. And don't think that you know it all. And there are warnings of this found in the Bible. Given by Solomon-Proverbs 3: 7; 26:12 . Also lamented by Isaiah-Isaiah 5:21. And also cautioned by Paul- 1 Corinthians 3:18. A renewed mind will maintain a strong sense of humility, an awareness that one has much to learn from God and others. We can possess a humble mind... just don't allow the devil to set you up with his playground of disbelief and slothfulness {laziness} in your mind.

How is it possible to retain a humbleness of mind? Hopefully, by reading and listening to the scriptures. Hopefully, aided by knowledge and experience. Often the more we learn, the more we realize how much we don't know. And hopefully by the example of Christ who was willing to submit to the will of his Father-John 6:38; 5:30. Who did not think so highly of Himself that he viewed equality with God something to be exploited- Philippians 2:6. Let me say this, adopting the mind of Christ will go a long way to helping maintain humility about ones self. Let me say to my Christian readers... let's stay humble in our minds and don't allow the enemy to set you up with his playgrounds within your mind to keep you back from reading, studying, praying and having humbleness of mind in Christ.

And in closing this chapter just remember the qualities of the renewed mind.

*Sameness of mind.

*Lowliness of mind.

*Humbleness of mind.

And remember the more that we adopt the mind of Christ, and make it our own the more we will think the same. The less we will be snobbish, and ambitious over the wrong things. The more we will associate with the less fortunate. The less conceited and arrogant we will be. For such are the qualities of those who have the mind of Christ, and are being transformed by the renewing of their minds. Are we setting our minds on things above, where Christ is (Colossians 3:1-2)? If we have been raised with Christ (via baptism, Colossians 2:12) that is our duty! And dear reader, if you have not been raised with Christ, why not today? Render it all over to Jesus in faith believing, repent of your sins, that you might begin to walk in the newness of Christ. Acts 2:38; Romans 6:3-4.

Don't allow another day for the devil to place his playgrounds of doubt within your mind. Tell him that your are being changed from the inside out. And from this moment forward you have a renewed mind in Jesus Christ. Old things are passed away and behold you are a new person in Christ Jesus .Give Jesus Praise for the victory over your life and mind.

Chapter Fifteen:
Developing The Mind Of Christ

1Corinthians 2:9-16... Read this passage of scripture before you go on reading the rest of this chapter in this book. And it will give you some insight on what is ahead in this chapter.

Let me ask you this question. What goes through your mind most days? How is your thinking? How is your thought life? Are you maintaining a positive, joyful, strong, pure perspective in the inner sanctuary of your mind? Or have you allowed the devil to set your mind up with his playground and inflicting you with "Stinking Thinking"? Do we need a check up from the neck up? Are your thoughts, thoughts of praise, purity, righteousness, victorious thoughts, spiritual thoughts? Or are they thoughts that are unholy and unhealthy? Thoughts of worry, anxiety, fear, vengeance, anger and hatred, criticism, discouraging, depressive, self-depreciating? If you are thinking these kind thoughts the enemy has set up his playground within your mind. Did you know that you and I are the product of our thinking? It says we are in Proverbs 23:27, "As a man thinks in his heart, so is he." So you and I are a product of our thoughts.

The word of God tells me in 1 Corinthians 2:13-16 that if we are born again, saved, and forgiven of our sins then we have the mind of Christ. Myself, I'm convinced that most of what you and I do is done out of habit rather than done because we thought it through. Let's not allow the devil to set up his playground of habits within our minds so that we don't think something through before we do it or say it. Then we'll be wishing that we never said it or did it!

My friends, there is a battle going on for the control of our minds! And whoever, or whatever, wins this battle for control in our thought life will ultimately win control of our entire life. And one of the process of developing our spiritual life is to bring our thought life into perfect obedience to our Lord Jesus Christ. So that we are not thinking: our thoughts, the world's thoughts, Satan's thoughts, thoughts that discourage and depress us, thoughts that tear us down, etc. We should grow consistently in thinking thoughts that are in line with the word and the will of God.

But I have good news for you today. You don't have to be controlled by negative, critical, depressive and discouraging thoughts that the devil is trying to use as his playground to get to you through your mind. I just want to share with you some of the good news form the bible, God's word. When you and I got saved--- God took up residence in our lives and because we are filled with the Holy Ghost. You and I now have the mind of Christ, therefore our lives are to be controlled by Christ. So I want to help you see how important your thought life is and help you understand how you can think God's thoughts, because as a Holy Ghost filled Saint of God you and I , we are to have the mind of Christ. The enemy need not even try and place his playground of thoughts within our mind because we are children of the Most High God.

Let's take a very close look at 1 Corinthians 2:16 once again. Did you see it? Did you see what it said? "For who has known the mind of the Lord that he may instruct Him? But we have the mind of Christ." Praise God! Do you believe that verse of scripture? The Bible says, we possess the mind of Christ. Did you know that the word of God has so much to say about our minds and our thought life? Here is a few of the many verses that speak to us about our minds and thought life. Isaiah 26:3 says, "Thou will keep him in perfect peace whose mind is stayed upon thee, because he trust in thee." Romans 12:2 says, "And be not conformed to this world: but be ye transformed by the renewing of your mind….." Romans 8:6 says, "For to be carnally minded is death; but to be spiritually minded is life and peace." Colossians 3:2 says, "Set your affections (mind) on things above." II Timothy 1:7 says, "God has given us the Spirit of a sound mind."

We must not allow the devil to set up his playgrounds within our minds and tell us anything different from what God's word is telling us. For God's word is truth! For John 17:17 says, "Sanctify them through thy truth: thy word is truth." So don't allow the devil to tell you anything different. For the word of God says, I have the mind of Christ and if I have the mind of Christ I have the victory in Jesus name! Right now… Give Jesus praise that you have the mind of Christ.

Our thought life is the most private and personal part of our entire life. There is no other person who knows our thoughts…except God. I'm sure a lot of you out there are really glad people don't know your thoughts! Let me say this, how would you like for everyone in your house to know exactly what you have been thinking of them for the past week? How about your boss? Your Pastor? While our thoughts are hidden from so many people around us… none of our thoughts are hidden from God? God knows everything we think. Every thought that passes through our mind, God knows about it. He knows every secret thought. David told his son Solomon, "Acknowledge the God your Father, and serve Him with wholehearted devotion and with a willing mind, for the Lord searches every heart and understands every motive behind every thought" 1 Chronicles 28:9.

It is my heart's prayer that everyone that is reading this book by the time that they finish it would be committed to a Spirit-controlled thought life. And committed to developing the mind of Christ. And committed to developing the character of God within us. And not to allow the devil to set up his playgrounds within your minds.

It does not matter how smart a person is. If they don't learn to start thinking spiritually and develop the mind of Christ…. then they are going to think some pretty stupid thoughts and develop some stupid ideas. 1 Corinthians 2:14, "The man without the Spirit does not accept the things that come from the Spirit of God, for they are foolishness to him, and he cannot understand them, because they are spiritually discerned." Develop the mind of Christ!

Here are several truths related to your mind and your thought life that I would like to share with my readers that I have discovered in the scriptures. Truths that concerns our mind. Most of the battles in our lives they are either won or lost in our mind. Romans 7:21-23 says, "I find then a law, that, when I would do good, evil is present with me. For I delight in the law of God after the inward man: But I see another law in my members, warring against the law of my mind, and bringing me into captivity to the law of sin which is in my members." My friends, defeat or victory is determined almost always in your mind.

Your battles with sin and Satan are won or lost in your mind. Let me say this, sin never begins as an action…. it begins as a thought. A thought that is a deceptive lie of Satan. A thought that you entertain, retain and eventually live/act out in action of your flesh. Satan plants a seed thought in our minds, one of his playgrounds, hoping that it will find a resting place in order to germinate and grow to produce a tree of destructive thoughts that will destroy our lives. We do not need to allow the devil to set up his playground of "stinking thinking" within our minds to the point that we entertain it. If you do entertain the thought for very long… it will lead eventually to bad behavior.

Saints of God, any true-life change begins with a transformed mind. Romans 12:2 says, "And be not conformed to this world: but be ye transformed by the renewing of your mind, that ye may prove what is that good, and acceptable, and perfect, will of God." Since most of the battles in our lives are won or lost in our mind, the key then to any true-life change is to have a mind that has been and is still in the process of being transformed by the power of God's word and His Spirit. The word "transformed" in Romans 12:2 comes from the word "metamorphosis." We need a metamorphosis in our thinking if we want any true-life change. And not allow the enemy to set up his playgrounds within our minds in any shape or form.

To change any habits or behaviors in our lives, we begin by letting God change our minds, our thinking. Our minds are being acted upon by the Holy Ghost to bring it into conformity with the will and word of God. The mind is not transforming itself- but is being transformed by the renewing processes of the Holy Spirit. (Renewal means to renovate, reshape or refashion). You and I need the Holy Spirit to renew, renovate, and refashion those evil, negative thought patterns that we have developed in our mind. Transformation of the mind is the work of the Holy Spirit. We need not allow the enemy to set up any playgrounds within our mind to keep us back from allowing the Holy Spirit to transform our minds to do the work that God has called us to do.

As Christians we need to have the mind of Christ operating in us for every decision we make, in every attitude we embrace, in every prayer we pray, in every observation we make, in every belief we adopt. That is what it means to have the mind of Christ. A lot of our problems are that we, more often than not, choose to listen and allow the devil to set up his playgrounds. Thus we listen to Satan and the world around us….instead of God's Spirit.

Or sometimes we listen to our own selfish flesh and embrace the thoughts that are contrary to the word and will of God. Thoughts that are destructive to the Christian life. It is very important that you and I live our life with a mind that has been transformed. A mind that no longer listens and believes Satan's lies which are all playgrounds of the mind to get use to lose out with God. But believe God's truth.

We must always choose between two opposing patterns of thought......Faith and Reason. Faith is God's way to live and think and reason is man's way to live and think. And the problem is that Faith and Reason are often in direct conflict with each other. And this does not mean that faith is unreasonable or illogical. We don't have to totally rid our brains to live by faith. In fact, if we had perfect, logic and reasoning abilities, we would always live in perfect agreement with God.

I want to now pursue what God has to say about developing the mind of Christ, and thinking God's thoughts. The importance of thinking God's thoughts. Did you know that our thinking affects every important area of our lives. Thinking God's thoughts affects our perspective. When we as Christians stop living by reason, and start living by faith with a transformed mind, the mind of Christ, it changes our perspective on every circumstance and situation we face. Your entire worldview will change when you have the mind of Christ and you are thinking the way God thinks.

This is why the devil tries his best to set us up with his playgrounds within our minds so that we will not have the mind of Christ and that we will not have the victory over the things that so easily beset us. Because when we have the mind of Christ the devil knows that he has lost the battle and we have gained the victory. If you and I can learn to think God's thoughts, it will give us a brand new, victorious, perspective on everything. Amen!

And if we will think God's thoughts it will affect our personality. The thought patterns you adopt are what eventually shapes and molds your personality. If we adopt thought patterns from the world, Satan, or our own self-centered desires, they will mold our personalities into selfish, difficult personality. In fact, all harmful personality quirks are the results of ungodly playground thought patterns that the devil has placed within your mind to keep you back from the blessings of God. We must not allow it. There are some who are reading this book who do not have a godly perspective and as a result, you have become negative, hostile and angry in your temperament. Please allow God to heal your mind of this playground that the devil has placed within you. When we begin to think God's thoughts, and adopt God's perspective on life.... it molds our personality into the likeness of Jesus Christ Himself.

2 Corinthians 5:17 says, "Therefore if any man be in Christ, he is a new creature: old things are passed away: behold, all things are become new." My friends, I am convinced, the more we think like Jesus- the more we will act like Him. If we would think Christ's thoughts it

would help sweeten some of our sour attitudes and change our bad temperament!

Thinking God's thoughts affects our priorities. When you and I have the mind of Christ, He begins to re-order our lives. First things will really become first. Jesus said in Matthew 6:33, "But seek ye first the kingdom of God, and his righteousness; and all these things shall be added unto you." The order will be reversed in your life without the mind of Christ. Right here is where you find so many Christians have such distorted priorities. A lot of people are living lives that are busy, but spiritually barren. Maybe most of us, desperately need the Lord Jesus to re-order our priorities by renewing our minds. We have bought in on values, ideals, and thought patterns that are imposed on us by the enemy and his playgrounds that he has placed within our minds, and not the Lord Jesus. And we must not allow this to happen in our lives.

Thinking God's thoughts affects our praying. Did you know that we can not pray effectively apart from the Holy Ghost and the mind of Christ? This is why most of our prayers are powerless! And this is why many of our prayers go unanswered. James 4:3 says, "Ye ask, and receive not, because ye ask amiss, that ye may consume it upon your lust." You may not be praying much with the mind of Christ, it could be that it is flesh-driven prayer and that is why your prayers are going unanswered. For this is a playground that the devil loves to set up in a lot of Christians minds, flesh-driven prayer and not praying with the mind of Christ.

Do you know how that you can get your prayers answered? By praying with the mind of Christ, under the direction of the Holy Spirit. Romans 8: 26-27 says, "Likewise the Spirit also helps our infirmities {weaknesses}: for we know not what we should pray for as we ought: but the Spirit itself makes intercession for us with groans which cannot be uttered. And he that searches the hearts knows what is the mind of the Spirit, because he makes intercession for the saints according to the will of God."

When you and I pray with the mind of Christ, we pray from an eternal perspective, rather than temporal. With God's glory as our ultimate desire. And with spiritual priorities, rather than material. We must not allow the devil to place his playgrounds within our minds concerning this area. For then, at that point, we lose out what God has for us through His Spirit directing us in what to pray about so that we can miss the mess or so that someone else will miss the mess.

What does it mean exactly to pray in Jesus name. For many Christians they think that the name of Jesus is some super password to get what they want from God. But praying in Jesus name means praying in concert with Christ's character and perfect will. Praying in Jesus name means praying from a position of unity, love and agreement with Jesus. Praying in Jesus name means praying with the mind of Christ, as you stand still in a relationship of union, love, and harmony with Jesus our Lord. John 14:13-14 says, "And whatsoever ye shall ask in my name, that will I do, that the Father may be glorified in the Son. If ye shall ask any thing in my name, I will do it."

As I close, I am wondering if any can hear what God may be saying to you in response to the writing of this book. Are you willing to submit your minds entirely to the Lord Jesus right now? I wonder how many that are reading this book would confess that you are losing a lot of spiritual battles in your mind because you have allowed the devil to place his playgrounds there to try and keep you back from receiving what Christ has for you? Just how many of you that have been reading this book are willing to confess that your life is being paralyzed by critical thoughts, depressive thoughts, negative thoughts, discouraging thoughts, angry and hostile thoughts? All these are playgrounds that the devil has been using on you to keep you back from receiving the blessings of God.

Are you willing to admit, that much of what you have been thinking about yourself, God and other people has been influenced by the playgrounds that the devil has set up within your mind to get you to believe a lie? Would you like to have the mind of the Lord Jesus Christ? Well, here is how. Begin by asking Jesus to come into your heart and save your soul. Then allow the mind of Christ to rule in your life. Apply what the word of God tells you and apply the teachings of this book to your life. Allow the Spirit of God to transform your mind by the renewing of your mind through the word of God. Read the bible daily, study it, pray daily to the Lord and you will have a Christ-like mind. Praise Him for the victory.

You may also buy my other book, "Be A God Pleaser: Take a Journey Through Biblical History" at www.authorhouse.com at their website's bookstore. This book will also help you become more like Christ and less like your old self. May God richly bless you all!

About The Author:

Pastor David L. Love began his ministry as an evangelist at the age of thirty-four in the State of Virginia in 1993 and experienced God's almighty hand at work through saving, healing, and delivering souls. In 1994 he was called to start a church in Crewe Virginia, Everlasting Faith Tabernacle. Today, as Pastor of New Harvest Church in the State of Montana and Co-Pastor and wife, Renee and nephew, Brad Love, Youth-Pastor and his wife Nicole, and the Pastor/Co-Pastor's son, Roy as Children's Minister. We all have a vision from God for the state and surrounding states and nations in and out of Montana to see souls saved. Pastor David L. Love currently resides in Livingston, MT with his wife Renee, son Roy and nephew Brad and his wife Nicole.

For information about New Harvest Church, visit website www.webspawner.com/users/newharvestchurch or email us at newharvestchurchmt@hotmail.com. Phone: 1-406-686-4180 Address: P.O. Box 576, Livingston, MT 59047.

Printed in the United States
41637LVS00006B/222

9 781420 829068